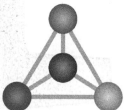

ENTERPRISE

CONNECTING THE DOTS™

www.PragmaticEA.com

Pragmatic Frameworks

A Pragmatic Introduction to PF2

v2021

Kevin Lee Smith

First published: August 2014
Last updated: January 2021

ISBN 978-1-908424-41-9 (hardback)
ISBN 978-1-908424-42-6 (paperback)
ISBN 978-1-908424-43-3 (ebook)

Published by:
Pragmatic365 Ltd
25 Buttermere
Great Notley,
Essex CM77 7UY
England

Currently Available Reference Books	ISBN	Pre-requisites
The Pragmatic Family of Frameworks A Pragmatic Introduction	978-1-908424-42-6	
Enterprise Fundamentals A Pragmatic Approach Using PEFF	978-1-908424-42-6	
Enterprise Transformation A Pragmatic Approach using POET	978-1-908424-07-5	PEFF
Enterprise Architecture A Pragmatic Approach using PEAF	978-1-908424-10-5	POET
Currently Available Focus Books	ISBN	Pre-requisites
PEAF 4 TOGAF Kick-start Your TOGAF Adoption. Pragmatically	978-1-908424-25-9	
Transformation Governance A Pragmatic Approach using Transformation Debt™	978-1-908424-48-8	
Enterprise Architecture Tools A Pragmatic Approach to EA Tool Selection and Adoption	978-1-908424-54-9	
What is EA A Pragmatic Explanation	978-1-908424-57-0	
Transformation Culture The Inconvenient Pragmatic Truth	978-1-908424-59-4	
Transformation Maturity Assessment A Pragmatic Approach using the PTMC	978-1-908424-63-1	
Connecting the DOTS™ The Death of "The Business" & "IT"	978-1-908424-68-6	
Coming Soon	ISBN	Pre-requisites
Enterprise Direction A Pragmatic Approach using POED	978-1-908424-16-7	PEFF
Enterprise Operation A Pragmatic Approach using POEO	978-1-908424-19-8	PEFF
Enterprise Support A Pragmatic Approach using POES	978-1-908424-22-8	PEFF
Enterprise Engineering A Pragmatic Approach using PEEF	978-1-908424-13-6	POET

This work was inspired by all those who seek to make the world a better place, rather than those who seek to own it.

"We cannot solve our problems,
with the same thinking we used when we created them."

Albert Einstein

"Sometimes it is the people who no one imagines anything of,
who do the things that no one can imagine."

Alan Turing

"Computers are useless.
They can only give you answers"

Pablo Picasso.

"You cannot 'cost justify' Architecture"

J. A. Zachman

"We have seen the enemy,
and the enemy is us (management)."

W. E. Deming

"If I have seen further,
it is by standing on the shoulders of giants."

Isaac Newton

Acknowledgements

The author would like to acknowledge the extensive help and advice provided by Murphy to get this book to market, particularly for the constant companionship and irritating interruptions (which provided much needed relief although I didn't know it at the time) and a chance for mutual tummy tickles.

I would also like to thank my wife, Virginia, for her moral support and the constant supply of Marmite on toast.

Please note that, to preserve commercial and personal confidentiality, any stories and examples in this book will usually have been adapted, combined and in part fictionalised from experiences in a variety of contexts, and do not and are not intended to represent any specific individual or Enterprise.

Registered trademarks such as PEAF, Zachman, TOGAF, ITIL, COBIT etc are acknowledged as the intellectual property of the respective owners.

Pragmatic thanks the following people who have contributed their ideas.

(In country alphabetical order)

If you would like to contribute ideas or have any comments or suggestions for improvements or corrections, please contact us.

| Australia | Hungary | New Zealand | United Kingdom | United Kingdom | United Kingdom | United States | United States | Zimbabwe |

Contributor	Area of Contributions
Taiss Quartapa Interim Executive Enlightened Interest Group **Australia**	Exploring the impossible is my calling. Whether that means working on the Enterprise Architecture, reinventing the internal processes of a global company or creating a new, innovative approach for the retail experience, solving the impossible is what I seek to do. I'm driven to deliver impactful results which enhance aspects of people's lives. POET > Culture > Slaves-to-Psychology > The-Dunning-Kruger-Effect
Tamás Nacsák Senior Enterprise Architect Telcotrend **Hungary**	Tamás Nacsák, is a Senior Enterprise Architect, worked twenty plus years in IT mostly in the telecommunication industry; the last twelve dedicated to Enterprise Architecture. He is currently working as Enterprise Architect on several Telco companies and at Hungarian State Tresury. POET > Culture > The-Architect > The-Pragmatic-Architect-Creed
Brendan S. McEnroe Chief Technology Officer // Enterprise Architect Trade Window Limited **New Zealand**	Brendan is a Certified Enterprise Architect, technology thought leader and start-up founder with 30 years' experience. He has a demonstrated history of digital strategy, innovation and leading high performing teams on large scale technology projects, across UK and NZ organisations. PEFF > Adoption > Measures > PTMC > Tools
Gareth Llewellyn Enterprise and Solution Architect Freelance **United Kingdom**	Over 28 years, Gareth has been a trusted advisor to executives and key decision makers. He has architected strategic transformations for medium to large commercial organisations, and to federal, state and local government across the UK and Australia. Gareth uses design thinking to transition businesses to their target operating model, delivering profound outcomes while reducing cost & risk. POET > Culture > The-Architect > What-Does-An-Architect-Do
Amber Smith Trainee Cabinetmaker Humphrey Munson **United Kingdom**	As someone who likes to learn, and loves a challenge, I have tried working in many different industries, some of which I loved, some I absolutely hated. I have come to know myself through trying new things. Recently, I have attained a job which I absolutely love, and aspire to turn into my career. Cabinetmaking allows me to be practical, creative, and keeps me on my toes! POET > Culture > Slaves-to-Psychology > The-Dunning-Kruger-Effect
Abdul Aziz Business Architect and Cybernetician Vanga Limited **United Kingdom**	A passionate strategist, enterprise architect and business change leader endeavouring to help executives, managers and operatives navigate complexity with principles and values that enable their organisational purpose. Abdul has over 20 years' experience in all aspects of "changing the business" across multiple industries holds an MBA with distinction from the Alliance Manchester Business School. POET > Culture > Architecture-and-Engineering > Fundamentals

James McGovern
Research Director
Gartner
United States

Over twenty years of experience applying technical, process, and people skills to improve individual, team, and organizational performance and overall efficacy. Advanced knowledge of enterprise architecture and enterprise security with a focus on high-profile customer-facing applications. An impassioned leader who mentors with purpose and understands that strong working relationships create great

PEAF > Culture > Roles > EASG-Enterprise-Architecture-Steering-Group

Pedro M. Correa
Harbinger of things to come
Papyrus Software
United States

Regional IT industry leader with SMET background and 25+ years of international experience in the Americas. Award winner for: leading regional sales and service delivery CoE while working as CTO (EDS), for Regional LATAM Sales/Marketing Director (Texas Instruments) and for Business Analyst/PMP (IBM)

PEAF > Methods > Phases > Roadmapping > Intermediate-Journey

Murambwa Clever Haparari
Technology Lead and Design Authority
FBC Holdings
Zimbabwe

Technology Innovation and Enterprise Architecture Leader with a vision to become an Enterprise Transformation leader driving Enterprises for the consistent achievement of their Strategic goals of Effectiveness, Efficiency, Agility and Sustainability of both the Operations and Transformation capabilities through appropriate adoption of the Enterprise Architecture Paradigm.

PEAF > Artefacts > Meta-models > Structural

Contents

FOREWORD

Enterprises have been and will continue to live in a state of flux. A never ending sea of change that buffets them and blows them around, seemingly at random, in an unending churning ocean. Even when it is calm, a storm can blow up "out of the blue" and literally sink the ship at a moment's notice. Most Enterprises invest huge amounts of time and effort in battling the storms. Very few spend any resources on preparing the ship. Instead the call is "all hands on deck" to land the next catch and set the next net. Without proper preparation, every Enterprise is sailing full speed into their own perfect storm.

If we are to sail safely in these unpredictable waters we must make preparations and plans to allow us to respond when treacherous conditions face us. For if we wait until that time before we act, it is unlikely that we will survive.

> "When you are drowning, it's too late to learn to swim."

While the seas are calm, an unprepared ship and crew is generally indistinguishable from a well prepared ship and crew. In fact the unprepared ship will often seem preferable to many, setting sail before other more well prepared ships - not having to waste time gathering and studying the correct charts, loading extra emergency rations, checking the presence and quality of the life-rafts nor performing preventative maintenance on the engine. Often the unprepared ship will set sail and return with a hold full of fish while the prepared ship is still making good their preparations.

The unprepared ship will often catch more fish than other more well prepared ships - not having to comply with safety regulations they are able to cast and wind in the nets much faster and therefore fill their holds faster. Holds also have more space due to the absence of emergency equipment which means more fish can be stored before having to return to port to offload them.

It is not a case of "if" the ship will meet the storm. It is a case of "when".

What preparations has your Enterprise made for its own "Perfect Storm"?

Kevin Lee Smith
The **Pragmatic** *Mariner*

Who Should Read This Book?

Anyone and everyone that is involved (in whole or in part) in the Strategising and Roadmapping phases of Enterprise Transformation (e.g. CxO's, Executive Management, Enterprise Architects, Strategic Transformation Planners, members of the PMO, etc.) and with the Governance and Lobbying of project execution (e.g. Project Managers, Business Analysts, Enterprise IT Architects, Solution Architects, Technical Architects, etc).

The book is intended for Enterprise Architects, Business Architects, IT Architects, process-designers and others who deal with the practical implications of whole-of-enterprise issues.

It should also be useful for Strategists and Service-managers, and for anyone else who works with other enterprise-wide themes such as supply-chains, value-webs, quality, security, knowledge-sharing, sustainability, business ethics and social responsibility, or health, safety and environment.

What Does This Book Tell Me?

PF2 provides a set of fundamental thoughts, ideas, definitions, ontologies and introduces the Pragmatic Family of Frameworks that use these things as their superclass.

The **Pragmatic** Family of Frameworks (**PF2**) is defined by its Mission Statement:

> "To provide Enterprises with **Pragmatic** frameworks to enable them to increase their maturity in how they fulfil their Mission"

This introduction to the **PF2** sets out the companies involved, the Licensing terms and what Training there is available. It also set out what frameworks are part of **PF2**, how they relate to each other, and how they relate to other frameworks,

KEYPOINT:

PF2 introduces the Companies and Frameworks that are part of the Pragmatic Family.

ADOPTION:

Management: Instigate a project to ensure everyone related to Transformation is trained in Pragmatic's Family of Frameworks.

Questions to Ponder

♦ What Frameworks does your Enterprise Use?

Introduction

KEYPOINT:

The Introduction section of PF2 introduces the companies that are part of the Pragmatic Family.

Questions to Ponder

♦ Do you think fundamental terminology is useful to your Enterprise?
♦ What fundamental terminology does your Enterprise use?
♦ If none, what fundamental terminology do you think would be appropriate?

Introduction > Companies

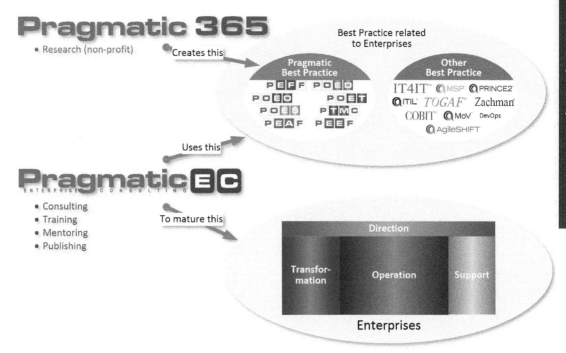

© Pragmatic 365 (2008-2021)

Pragmatic 365 is a non-profit research company (hereinafter referred to as **Pragmatic**) dedicated to developing Best Practice in relation to the structure and transformation of Enterprises. All profits are poured back into the continuous evolution and creation of best practice. This best practice, contributes to the existing best practice in the marketplace, such as PRINCE2, MSP, TOGAF, etc. Pragmatic is tracking over 900 frameworks currently in the marketplace.

Pragmatic EC is a consulting company which uses any appropriate Best Practice (whether developed by **Pragmatic** or not) to help Enterprises mature any or all parts of their Transformation Capability (from Strategy to Deployment). This is done by consulting, training, mentoring and publishing.

Pragmatic EC is unique, because it's domain of excellence is, **HOW** Enterprises effect Transformation not the doing Transformation. That is, our mission is to help Enterprises mature their Transformation capability, not their Operations capability. This contrasts with almost all other consultancies, which concentrate on improving the Operations part of Enterprises, and as such have people who are experts in various business verticals such as Financial, Pharma, Energy, Health, etc.

Pragmatic EC can work with Enterprises in any business vertical, since the fundamentals of an Enterprises Transformation capability, is not dependant upon the type of Business they are in. The way that HR or Finance is carried out, is fundamentally the same in all Enterprises. So, the way Transformation is carried out (or rather should be carried out) is the same in all Enterprises. The output of HR, Finance and Transformation may be directed towards a specific business vertical, but the fundamentals of HR, Finance and Transformation are the same for all.

Our centre of excellence is therefore…

The Transformation of Transformation.

> ## KEYPOINT:
>
> Pragmatic 365 is a non-profit research company. Pragmatic EC is a consulting company.

> ## ADOPTION:
>
> Management: Engage Pragmatic EC to assess and help you to mature your Enterprise's Transformation capability.

Questions to Ponder

♦ What Companies do you know of, that create best practice relating to Enterprise Transformation?

♦ What Consultancies do you know of, that are focussed on the Transformation of Transformation, rather than the Transformation of Operations?

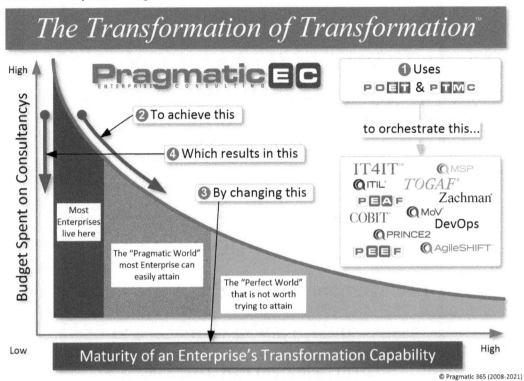

Most consultancies won't tell you what **Pragmatic** will tell you.

Most consultancy's revenue streams, are *inversely* proportional to how mature their client's Transformation Capability is. Most consultancies are therefore motivated, NOT to mature an Enterprise's Transformation Capability. The more immature an Enterprise's Transformation Capability is, the more money the consultancy is likely to make, in fixing all the problems that will arise. Have you ever wondered why the "70% of all project fail" statistic hasn't changed for 40 years? Now you know!

Because most Enterprises primary function and expertise is NOT in relation to Transformation, they tend to live in the Red area depicted on the graph. Their Transformation capabilities are barely mature enough to effect the transformation they require, and the result is missed deadlines, blown budgets, unfulfilled customer expectations, and as a result, large consultancy bills.

The green area illustrates a "perfect world" where the Enterprise is supremely mature in its Transformation capability. There is little reason to try to attain such levels of maturity as the law of diminishing returns applies.

The yellow area indicates the sweet spot, where the level of maturity is both appropriate and attainable.

Pragmatic is different from almost all other consultancies. We concentrate on enabling Enterprises to move from the Red area to the Yellow area. This is achieved by:

1) Utilising POET and the PTMC to orchestrate Best Practice...
2) To move an Enterprise's Transformation capability from the red to the yellow...
3) Which is accomplished by increasing the maturity of an Enterprises Transformation capability...
4) Which results in a large decrease in the time and money spent on Consultancies.

We believe that anything that can be done to reduce an Enterprise's reliance on external consultancies (and their associated costs and risks) is a good thing.

Pragmatic's Mission is...

> "To provide Enterprises with Pragmatic frameworks to enable them to increase their maturity in HOW they effect Transformation/Change"

Pragmatic's Vision is...

> "The Transformation of Transformation."

KEYPOINT:

Most consultancies only want to sell you fish.

Pragmatic will teach you how to fish.

ADOPTION:

Management: Engage Pragmatic EC to help you reign in the budget spent on consultancies and therefore Transformation.

Questions to Ponder

- Which consultancies do you know of, which help you improve HOW you do Transformation vs those that just want to help you DO Transformation?
- How much could you reduce your annual Transformation budget by, if you matured HOW you do Transformation?

Introduction

✓ **350 Companies**

✓ **130 Government Bodies**

✓ **60 Academic Institutions**

✓ **3,700 Individuals**

✓ **43 Consultancies**

✓ **13 Training Providers**

✓ **11 Tool Vendors**

As at Q1/2021

© Pragmatic 365 (2008-2021)

Non-Commercial (Internal)

If you wish to use any of **Pragmatic**'s Ontologies, Frameworks or materials (in whole or in part) internally, that is, to improve the Transformation Capability of your Enterprise, then your Enterprise, and the people that use them, only require a Non-Commercial License.

The **Pragmatic** Non-Commercial license is issued FREE and is automatically renewed for FREE on an annual basis.

The license is issued with the following terms:

♦ Any use must be attributable to **Pragmatic 365**.

♦ Details of the license issued will be posted on the **Pragmatic 365** website.

♦ **Pragmatic's** Ontologies, Frameworks or materials cannot be used for profit externally.

♦ The Licensee is entitled to use the Licensee Logo on promotional materials.

♦ When used on a website the logo must link back to www.Pragmatic365.org

♦ Licensees agree to be contacted by **Pragmatic 365** periodically with updates.

Applications for a license can be made at http://www.Pragmatic365.org/licensing-non-commercial.asp

Commercial (External)

If you wish to use any of **Pragmatic's** Ontologies, Frameworks or materials (in whole or in part) externally, that is, to improve the Transformation Capability of your clients Enterprises (not your own) (e.g. Consultancies, Training Providers and Tool Vendors), then your Enterprise, and the people that use them, must possess a Commercial License.

> **NOTE:** Contractors who operate their own one-man-band companies and provide services through recruitment agencies to End-User Organisations and Government Bodies are not considered to be consultancies and therefore only require a Non-Commercial License.

If you wish to evaluate any of **Pragmatic's** Ontologies, Frameworks or materials internally for commercial use, you can do so under a free Non-Commercial License.

If you wish to evaluate any of **Pragmatic's** Ontologies, Frameworks or materials for external commercial use (by using it with an external client) this is possible by contacting **Pragmatic** first and obtaining written permission to do so.

The license is issued with the following terms:

- Any use must be attributable to **Pragmatic 365**.
- Details of the license issued will be posted on the **Pragmatic 365** website.
- **Pragmatic's** Ontologies, Frameworks or materials can be used for profit externally.
- The Licensee is entitled to use the Licensee Logo on their websites and other promotional materials.
- When used on a website the logo must link back to www.Pragmatic365.org
- Licensees agree to be contacted by **Pragmatic 365** periodically with updates.
- It is expressly forbidden to pass on any **Pragmatic** Commercial Licensing Fees to clients of the commercial Enterprise, either directly or indirectly.
- The Standard Commercial License specifically prohibits the production of derivative frameworks, however, if you wish to create derivative frameworks this is possible by contacting **Pragmatic 365** and obtaining explicit written consent.

To apply for a license, please see http://www.Pragmatic365.org/licensing-commercial.asp

> # KEYPOINT:
>
> Use Pragmatic Frameworks (for free) to improve your Enterprise.

> # ADOPTION:
>
> Management: Apply for a Pragmatic Commercial or Non-Commercial license depending on your circumstances.

Questions to Ponder

♦ Which License is best for you?

Introduction > Training > Certification Courses

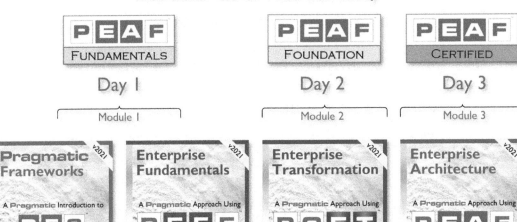

© Pragmatic 365 (2008-2021)

There are three levels which build toward PEAF Certified status. PEAF Fundamentals training is a pre-requisite for PEAF Foundation training is a pre-requisite for PEAF Certified training, because PEAF inherits and builds on the **Pragmatic** Operating model for Enterprise Transformation defined by POET which in turn inherits and builds on the **Pragmatic** Enterprise Fundamentals Framework.

These courses educate individuals and Enterprises in a vendor and technology neutral **Pragmatic** approach to improving their Transformation capability in general and the Enterprise Architecture part of that domain, in particular.

You can choose from Self-Study or Instructor led formats.

♦ **Self Study Training** is **FREE** and is split into three modules. Each module corresponds to the content taught in the classroom. You can stop and start whenever you like. To move on to the next Module, you must pass all preceding exams. How long you take to study and how often you take the exams is completely up to you. You only pay for certification exams if you want to take them.

♦ **Instructor led Training and Certification** is fee based, and run by a **Pragmatic 365** Certified Trainer. Each day consists of 6 hours of presentation and discussions, finishing with a 1 hour Exam.

In addition, **Pragmatic** also offers various 1 day workshops targeted at specific subject areas.

Certification Courses

- ◆ **PEAF Fundamentals** (1 day) sets out the basic language and ontologies used throughout all **Pragmatic**'s Frameworks.
- ◆ **PEAF Foundation** (1 day) sets out an Operating Model for the whole of the transformation domain (from Strategy to Deployment) and the common patterns of methods and artefacts that allow an organisation to tactically improve parts of it while preserving the effectiveness and efficiency of the whole. It sets the context for Enterprise Architecture in terms of where it fits in, and where it doesn't.
- ◆ **PEAF Certified** (1 days) concentrates on the specifics of the EA domain and sets out the fundamental pieces to be put in place to be successful.

Certification Exams

- • Exams are marked dynamically in real-time, and so if you get an answer wrong or partially wrong, you will receive feedback for example "Correct but you need to give a little more detail".
- • The pass mark for all exams is 100%. The reason for this is that we want to make sure that people understand 100% of the things an exam is asking (which is only a small proportion of the entire content).
- • Most people complete each exam in **45-60** minutes, and although there is no hard time limit as such, we will close each exam after 2 hours.
- • If you fail an exam, you are welcome to re-sit the exam (maximum of 3 times) at a later time for no additional cost

Target Audience

The course is suitable for anyone who is interested in maturing **how** Transformation and change is effected within an Enterprise and how Enterprise Architecture fits in and helps with that.

Prior Knowledge

No prior knowledge of Enterprise Architecture is required, although it is useful if the attendees have worked as part of the Transformation capability of an Enterprise.

Relevant Industries.

Learning the fundamental discipline of Enterprise Architecture (and the wider Transformation domain) and how to mature it in an Enterprise is not dependent upon any business industry knowledge.

Previous Customers

Experian, Hasbro, Freshfields Bruckhaus Deringer, California Franchise Tax Board, California Department of Health Care Services, Aspen Re, Dunn & Bradstreet, California State Board of Equalization.

Private/On Site Courses

Can be run and tailored to the challenges of your Enterprise.

Certification Body

The certificating body is **Pragmatic 365** Ltd. A Non-Profit.

Previous comments

We have a 100% positive feedback from the course. Some comments below but all comments (unedited and unabridged) can be read at www.pragmatic365.org/credibility-comments-training.asp

"Excellent, thought provoking and well laid out"

- Global Automation Manager, UK

"Energizing and invigorating -- helps put the passion back in EA efforts"

- VP Marketing & Business Development, USA

"It was fantastic course - very insigthful and valuable. Thank you."

- Architect, UK

"A refreshing approach to EA, focused on *helping* the business develop an approach and strategy, rather than telling them what to do. The course was very logical and easy to follow."

- Executive Director, USA

Do people recommend PEAF?

92% of people would recommend PEAF to others. Some comments are show below but all comments (unedited and unabridged) can be read at www.pragmatic365.org/credibility-comments-survey.asp

"I would recommend PEAF because PEAF has a down to earth holistic enterprise approach that makes EA goals and approach understandable by stakeholders, management and practitioners"

- EA, Independent EA, Greece

"I would recommend PEAF because It is a great straight forward place to start looking into EA. The concept are straightforward and both easy to apply and understand."

- ICT Architect, Australia

"I would recommend PEAF because of it's logical and Pragmatic approach to EA. I find it less academic than some of the other frameworks."

- Enterprise Solution Architect, South Africa

"I would recommend PEAF because a) Provides a good roadmap for transformation b) Vendor and technology neutral c) Simplifies the EA artefacts d) Most comprehensive framework"

- Consultant, India

> # KEYPOINT:
>
> PEAF Certified training, provides everything to enable you to adopt PEAF.

> # ADOPTION:
>
> Management: Engage Pragmatic EC to deliver PEAF Certified Transformation Best Practice training.

Questions to Ponder

- Have you read any of these books?
- If so, what did you like? What did you not like?
- Have you been on any of these courses?
- If so, what did you like? What did you not like?
- Which course would interest you the most?

Introduction > Training > Focused Workshops

Various workshops are available based on specially selected content from the base PEFF/POET/PEAF material, which focuses on particular areas of concern.

You can choose from Self-Study or Instructor led formats.

♦ **Self Study Training** is **FREE** although obviously does not provide people with the workshop type of environment that allows for specific issues to be discussed. However, Self Studying this content does work towards your PEAF certification if you decide to go that way in the future.

♦ **Instructor Workshops** are fee based, and run by a **Pragmatic 365** Certified Consultant. As well as covering the content, there is also time for discussions about applying the content to your specific context.

PEAF 4 TOGAF

Why Should I Read This Book?

TOGAF® is a well known and "popular" Framework...

"CERTIFICATION PASSES 100,000 MILESTONE"

- blog.opengroup.org/2020/06/23/togaf-9-certification-passes-100000-milestone

But while there are many thousands of people certified in it, the number of people and Enterprises that actually use it, is much much lower. A lot of that has to do with the "badge appeal" in that it is something that people like to see on a CV, but a lot of it also has to do with the difficulty in adopting it. While TOGAF's strength lies in its detail, so does its weakness. PEAF strengths lies in its **Pragmatism**.

Who Should Read This Book?

Anyone who has taken TOGAF training and wants to use PEAF to Pragmatically adopt it, from CxO's and Directors to Database Support technicians. From Project Managers to Business Analysts. From Management Consultants to Programmers, and any one of a thousand other job titles that are (in whole or in part) concerned with the Transformation of Enterprises.

Why Should I attend a Workshop?

Run over 1 day and using this book, this Workshop introduces you to the parts of PEAF that can most pragmatically aid your adoption of TOGAF. Each part is mapped to the TOGAF sections and ADM allowing attendees to easily move between PEAF and TOGAF and vice versa.

If you have been on a TOGAF® workshop and are now wondering what to do, This workshop can help you.

This Workshop will provide you with the context and approach to give you that best chance of success.

Enterprise Transformation Assessment

Why Should I Read This Book?

Enterprises (Public Companies, Private Companies, Government Agencies) spend a lot of time and money on Transformation initiatives, however, most spend very little (if any) time and money on the MAGIC used. This lack of Transformation focus contributes to the widely accepted figures that 70% of all projects fail.

In the 21st Century, it is no longer enough just to be able to change. What matters now is how effective and efficient an Enterprise is at planning and executing that change. How an Enterprise effects Transformation has become a Strategic Strength where massive business opportunities can be gained, or a Strategic Weakness where massive business problems will result.

The **Pragmatic** Transformation Maturity Canvas (PTMC) Workshop is designed to enable Enterprises to effectively and efficiently perform a very **Pragmatic** maturity assessment of their Enterprise Transformation Capability.

Who Should Read This Book?

Anyone and everyone that is involved (in whole or in part) in the Transformation of Enterprises, from CxO's and Directors to Database Support technicians. From Project Managers to Business Analysts. From Management Consultants to Programmers, and any one of a thousand other job titles that are (in whole or in part) concerned with the Transformation of Enterprises.

Why Should I attend a Workshop?

Run over 1 day and using this book, the first part of the workshop presents the concepts required to understand the PTMC and why considering the maturity of your Enterprise Transformation capability is strategically important to its continued survival.

The remainder of the day is a hands-on workshop attendees use the PTMC to begin to consider and then expose the maturity of their Enterprise Transformation capability, and to develop overall findings and recommendations for its maturation.

Your Enterprises Transformation capability is strategically important to its survival.

This Workshop will provide you with an approach to assess it, and give you the best chance of maturing it in a **Pragmatic** way.

The Death of the Business and IT

Why Should I Read This Book?

Most Enterprises organise themselves around the tried and tested "Business" and "IT" way of thinking, and their departments and CxOs. This is understandable and has served us well over the years. However, this paradigm is no longer appropriate.

Who Should Read This Book?

Anyone and everyone that is involved (in whole or in part) in the Transformation of Enterprises, from CxO's and Directors to Database Support technicians. From Project Managers to Business Analysts. From Management Consultants to Programmers, and any one of a thousand other job titles that are (in whole or in part) concerned with the Transformation of Enterprises.

Why Should I attend a Workshop?

In the 21st century, the "IT" of an Enterprise is so inextricably linked to "The Business" of an Enterprise, it is impossible to decide where "The Business" stops and "IT" begins. In fact for many Enterprises today, "IT" is the business to a large extent. So, does this mean handing over the management and direction of the Enterprise to "IT"? No. that would be ludicrous, but so is thinking in terms of "The Business" and "IT". So what do we do? How can we square this circle? How can we think and organise enterprises in the 21st Century? The answer is to think in terms of Connecting the DOTS™

Run over 1 day and using this book, this workshop presents and defines DOTS. It discusses why thinking in terms of "The Business" and "IT" is no longer appropriate, and why adopting DOTS can ensure an Enterprise concentrates on, and be driven by, the core strategic capabilities of any Enterprise.

If you wish to make sure your Enterprise can excel in the 21st century, it is imperative that it focusses on its key strategic capabilities.

This workshop will provide you with the context and approach to give you that best chance of success.

Enterprise Transformation Governance

Why Should I Read This Book?

Many Enterprises already have some kind of governance with respect to Enterprise Transformation. Sadly, many of the Methods (and Artefacts) employed are deeply flawed. Governance tends to be either a tick in the box exercise or a policing exercise. Having witnessed the failure of many Transformation/change initiatives over 35 years, I have created a new way of effecting Governance, with addition of the crucial Lobbying component that is missing in most Enterprises. The changes required to utilise Enterprise Debt™ are small but the effects can be truly game changing. If the Management decides to control (manage) Transformation Debt™, then this book sets out all that is required to do so. Pragmatically.

Enterprises (Public Companies, Private Companies, Government Agencies) spend Billions of Dollars year on year Transforming and changing themselves. With widely accepted figures of 70% of all projects fail (McKinsey, September 2013) the amount of money (and more importantly time) that is lost cannot continue, especially in a world that is changing faster and faster while demanding that all this Transformation must be done with less resource.

Identifying and managing Transformation Debt™ (that is created when Transformation work deviates from accepted Roadmaps and Principles) is the key to keeping your Transformation projects aligned with your Strategy and identifying when any deviations occur at the point when that deviation occurs so that sound business decisions can me made to either accept the deviation with a plan of how to deal with the resulting issues and risks, or to act to stop the deviation.

Who Should Read This Book?

Anyone who wants to stop wasting time and money and reduce the number of project failures. E.g. CIOs, Head of PMO, Head of Business Analysis, Head of S&A, Head of Solution Delivery, Enterprise Architects, Solution Architects, Business Analysts, Project Managers, Developers, Testers, Configuration Managers, Change Managers, etc, etc.

Why Should I attend a Workshop?

Pragmatic Approach to Enterprise Transformation Governance.

Run over 1 day and using this book, the first part of the workshop presents the concepts required to understand Transformation Debt™ and provides a detailed method for defining, measuring and managing it.

The remainder of the day is a hands-on workshop where you will think about the principles that are applicable to your Enterprise, practise defining the Transformation Debt™ when those principles are violated, and making decisions to accept the debt created or provide the resources required.

Transformation Debt™ is a fact.

Your Transformation efforts are creating it every day.

Either you will control it.

Or it will control you.

Enterprise Transformation Culture

Why Should I Read This Book?

Enterprises (Public Companies, Private Companies, Government Agencies) spend a lot of money on Transformation initiatives, and in trying to mature how they plan and execute those initiatives. A lot of time and money is spent on processes and IT tools to help an Enterprise plan and run projects better. However, after all this time and money is spent, processes are changed, new tools are bought and installed, still the overall numbers are that 70% of all projects fail. How can this be? The simple answer is that the culture at large in most Enterprise Transformation capabilities (the unwritten rules and regulations) are perfectly engineered to produce a 70% failure rate. So put away your tools, and start thinking about culture today.

Culture trumps Everything™ is much much more than just a saying. It is a very cold hard fact, which if ignored, literally has the capacity to destroy civilisations.

Who Should Read This Book?

Anyone and everyone that is involved (in whole or in part) in the Transformation of Enterprises, from CxO's and Directors to Database Support technicians. From Project Managers to Business Analysts. From Management Consultants to Programmers, and any one of a thousand other job titles that are (in whole or in part) concerned with the Transformation of Enterprises.

Why Should I attend a Workshop?

Run over 1 day and using this book, the workshop exposes the culture that exists in many enterprises. It gets the attendees thinking in terms of culture, different ways to think about it, the role psychology plays, how the two tribes of "the business" and "IT" contrast, and over 40 keypoints to help focus the mind.

Your Enterprise is already spending a lot of money on Transformation initiatives, and so it is imperative that your Enterprise stands the best chance of reducing the 70% failure rate.

This Workshop will provide you with the context and approach to give you that best chance of success.

Enterprise Architecture Tools

Why Should I Read This Book?

Many Enterprises already have some kind of EA Modelling Tool, that are being actively used for the purpose of Enterprise Architecture, aka creating and maintaining Structural (Capability) and Transformational (Portfolio) Roadmaps. But those Enterprises are in the minority.

Many, many more have either no EA Modelling Tool at all, or they have one but have found that it has not lived up to expectations and sits gathering dust on the shelf or being used as glorified reporting tool and generally providing questionable (if any) returns.

Having witnessed many failures, this book sets out the Methods, Artefacts and Environment required to effectively choose and operate an EA Modelling Tool. It covers the key things that must be done to effectively and efficiently choose a tool, and then to operate it in a sustainable way.

If the Management decides to choose (or replace) and operate an EA modelling tool effectively, then this book sets out all that is required to do so. Pragmatically.

Who Should Read This Book?

Anyone involved in making sure their investment in an EA Modelling Tool is sound. E.g. CIOs, Head of PMO, Head of Business Analysis, Head of S&A, Head of Solution Delivery, Enterprise Architects, Solution Architects, Business Analysts, Project Managers, Configuration Managers, Change Managers, etc, etc.

Why Should I attend a Workshop?

Run over 1 day and using this book, the first part of the workshop presents the concepts required to understand an EA Modelling Tool, what it used for, what information must be modelled, and **Pragmatic** methods for adoption and use.

The remainder of the day is a hands-on workshop where you will formulate your own tailored approach for selection, define which requirements are key to you, and develop a shortlist.

Enterprises (Public Companies, Private Companies, Government Agencies) spend a lot of time and money on tools. But many of these tools sit on the shelf or are used in only small ways.

The most common reasons are that:

The tool they selected is not is not appropriate for their Enterprise.

The way the tool is being used is not appropriate for their Enterprise.

> ### If you are going to be spending a lot of money on a tool, it is imperative that the project stands the best chance of success.

> ## This Workshop will provide you with the context and approach to give you that best chance of success.

What is Enterprise Architecture

Why Should I Read This Book?

Enterprises (Public Companies, Private Companies, Government Agencies) spend a lot of money on Enterprise Architecture. But the world is so full of myths, half-truths and misinterpretations, they rarely get to understand what it actually is, much less how to use it. EA has the capacity to massively increase the effectiveness, efficiency, agility and sustainability of an Enterprises transformation portfolio.

Enterprise Architecture has existed (in many forms) for a long time, and there are many "experts" around to educate others. However, EA is currently at the same point in time, as Chemistry was when Chemists were Alchemists. So perhaps a better term for Enterprise Architecture is Enterprise Alchemy and a better term for Enterprise Architects is Enterprise Alchemists. (It is perhaps serendipitous that the acronym is the same!)) The parallels between what EA claims and what alchemy claimed are intriguing.

That may see flippant or a pathetic attempt at humour, however, in admitting that, as a profession, EA is about as mature as alchemy was hundreds of years ago, we have made the most important step of all. The first step. We have stopped being unconsciously incompetent and we are now concisely incompetent. Admitting that EA is as mature as Alchemy is big thing. Many people will not agree (mostly the Alchemists!). Many people have a vested interest in presenting themselves and their companies as "experts" even when their expertise just turns out to be "whatever we think".

The time has come for a change. The time has come for Enterprise Alchemy to grow up and Become Enterprise Architecture. This book presents information to define Enterprise Architecture, and Architects in a Pragmatic fashion. It does not purport to be the end of the road. But it does try to be the beginning.

Who Should Read This Book?

Anyone and everyone that is involved (in whole or in part) in the Transformation of Enterprises, from CxO's and Directors to Database Support technicians. From Project Managers to Business Analysts. From Management Consultants to Programmers, and any one of a thousand other job titles that are (in whole or in part) concerned with the Transformation of Enterprises.

Why Should I attend a Workshop?

Run over 1 day and using this book, the workshop presents what EA is (the noun and the verb), what EA is not (the noun and the verb), how EA fits into the wider Transformation domain, how the popular frameworks such as Zachman, TOGAF, POET, PEAF, COBIT and ITIL fit in, the fundamental differences between Architecture & Engineering, the two types of Enterprise Architect (the role) and over 50 keypoints to help focus the mind.

> ### If you are going to be spending a lot of money on EA, it is imperative that your Enterprise stands the best chance of success.
>
> ### This Workshop will provide you with the context and approach to give you that best chance of success.

Introduction

> ## KEYPOINT:
> PEAF Focused Workshops, allow you to focus on specific areas.

> ## ADOPTION:
> Management: Engage Pragmatic EC to deliver Focussed training.

Questions to Ponder

- ♦ Have you read any of these books?
- ♦ If so, what did you like? What did you not like?
- ♦ Have you been on any of these workshops?
- ♦ If so, what did you like? What did you not like?
- ♦ Which course would interest you the most?

Introduction > Training > Options

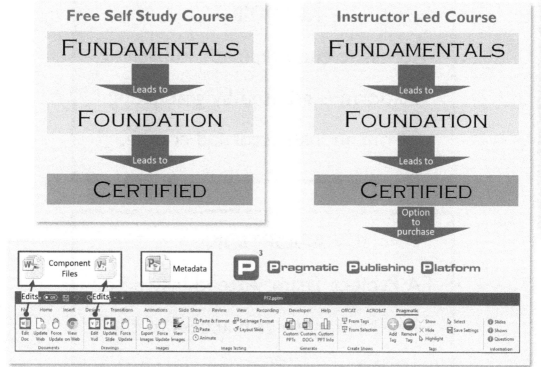

© Pragmatic 365 (2008-2021)

The progression from Fundamentals through Foundation to Certified is the same for people opting for Self Study or Instructor Led training.

In addition, Enterprises that have completed the Instructor Led course are also able to buy (as an option) the **Pragmatic Publishing Platform (P3)**, to allow them to create and modify Frameworks in an efficient and seamless way.

Introduction

> # KEYPOINT:
>
> Access to the Pragmatic Publishing Platform is granted by graduating from an Instructor led course.

> # ADOPTION:
>
> EA Project Team: Attend Instructor led training, to gain access to the Publishing Platform and all component files.files.

Questions to Ponder

- ◆ Which type of course would you choose?
- ◆ Do you think a better understanding could be gained from an Instructor led course?
- ◆ What are the benefits of each type of course?

Introduction > Pragmatic Publishing Platform

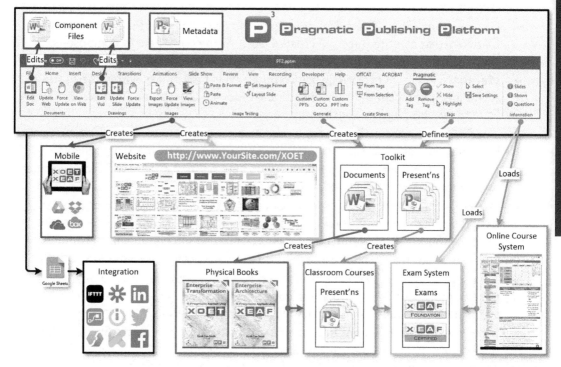

© Pragmatic 365 (2008-2021)

The **Pragmatic Publishing Platform** (**P3**) is available for purchase separately and exists in two versions:

- ◆ A **Standalone Version** – with no content, allowing people to create and maintain any content they wish, that results in the creation of training presentations, associated exams, websites and books.
- ◆ A **Pragmatic Version** – which include 100% of the base material in all of **Pragmatic** frameworks – currently PF2, POET and PEAF, allowing people to rebrand and modify as they wish.

P3 comprises a coherent environment which automates much of the administrative tasks related to the production and maintenance of the base material and the creation of custom material. The platform uses MS PowerPoint as its base, utilising a custom **Pragmatic** Ribbon to allow users to manage the material.

- ◆ **Documents** – Allow the maintenance of the words for each component.
- ◆ **Drawings – Allow the maintenance of the drawings for each component.**
- ◆ **Images – Allows the generation of images.** Separate .png files are exported in five different resolutions - one for Books, three for the website (thumbnail, normal and hi-res) and one for the export folder.
- ◆ **Image Testing – Allows supplementary functions for testing image generation.**
- ◆ **Generate - Allow the generation of PowerPoint and Word Toolkit documents**
- ◆ **Create Shows – Allows the creation of shows using tags or the selection**

- **Tags – Allows the manipulation and visualisation of tags which define each show.**
- **Component Files-** These files constitute the master files of the Framework or Ontology that all other files are created from. Each component is composed of a Visio file for the graphic and a Word document for the words.
- **Metadata** – This information (per component) is held in tags within the Notes of each slide. It comprises Show indicators, Keypoints, Questions, Answers, Adoption Statements and Reader Questions.
- **Toolkit** – From these Components, any number of Documents and PowerPoint Presentations can be easily created, based on a selection of the Components.
- **Website** - Easily integrate your framework (images and words) with your intranet to promote understanding and adoption.
- **Mobile** - The images of your framework are automatically exported to a folder (e.g. Dropbox) that can be synchronised to mobile devices, allowing you to carry the core of your framework with you at all times, to promote understanding and adoption.
- **Books** – From the Book documents, physical books can be easily created.
- **Training Courses** – Training courses consisting of presentations to be used in classroom training and information loaded into an online course system. In addition an online examination system is loaded with exam questions.
- **Integration** – Component Information is synchronised to Google Sheets, which can then in turn, integrate though any integration application to, for example, Facebook, Twitter, LinkedIn etc for publishing of changes or daily messages.

> ## KEYPOINT:
>
> P3 allows Enterprises to easily produce and maintain their own Frameworks and publish them to books, their intranet and mobile devices.

> ## ADOPTION:
>
> Management: Adopt the Pragmatic Publishing Platform to streamline your Pragmatic X-Framework adoption.

Questions to Ponder

- What do you currently use to maintain and publish the frameworks your Enterprise uses?
- What other uses can you think of for the Pragmatic Publishing Platform?

Introduction

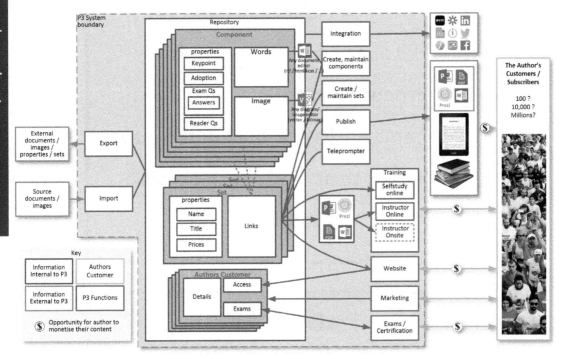

© Pragmatic 365 (2008-2021)

P3 is a component-based knowledge authoring and publishing system. All content is constructed from components. A component is whatever the author wants a component to be, however it is suggested that each component teach people one important concept or thing. More complicated things should be broken down into other components. Each component consists of three distinct pieces of information:

♦ **Words** – Authored in any document editor such as Microsoft Word, and in any format such as rtf or html.

♦ **Images** – Authored in any image editor such as Visio, and in any format such as raster (e.g. png, gif, jpg) or vector (e.g. vsd, wmf)

♦ **Properties**

    ♦ Name (as part of a navigation structure)

    ♦ Keypoint – The key thought or point that the reader should take away from this component.

    ♦ Adoption – A list of things to do in order to adopt the component.

    ♦ Exam Questions – One or more exam questions to test the knowledge of someone learning the component.

    ♦ Exam Answers – For each question, I correct answer and any number of wrong answers, to allow a multiple choice examination to be conducted. (The exam subsystem allows for both multiple choice exams and written exams)

In addition, the repository contains two other important parts.

Firstly Sets. Sets collect components together for the purposes of publishing and training.

- Links – a list of links to components included in the set and the order that is required.
- Properties
    - Name – The Authors internal quick name of the set
    - Title – The title to be used when published
    - Prices – The prices of things published for example print books, Kindle books, training courses.

Secondly, Authors Customer.

- Details - Information about the authors customers/subscribers, such as name, email address etc.
- Access – Information about what content the authors customer has accessed and when.
- Exams – Information about what courses and exams the user has subscribed to.

All of this information is owned and controlled by the Author and can be exported at any time, in a variety of formats (words documents, image files, sets, etc) such that the Author always owns their content.

In addition, to aid adoption of the platform, Authors can import their existing knowledge in a variety of formats with automatic splitting of large documents into components by using some identifying data such as headings or page breaks.

- Functionality
- Integration
- Create, Maintain, Components
- Create, Maintain Sets
- Publish
- Training
- Website
- Marketing
- Exams / Certification

Customer Segments

- Worldwide - Platform akin to YouTube for thinkers.
    - Best practice
    - Stories for children/learning
- Companies – To document the MAGIC of their business, for onboarding or general change management teaching/rollout.
- Universities - For professors to author content for students.

Why would an author want to use P3?

People who tick 1 or more of these boxes:

- Have a reasonably large set of information/knowledge
- Need flexibility to easily evolve/maintain it over time
- Want to share/publish their content on the internet/intranet
- Want to publish their content to eBook or Print
- Want to be able to easily slice and dice their content into focus areas.
- Want to offer training (offline, online, onsite) to people.
- Want to offer exams/certification to people.
- Want to automatically push their content out via twitter, likedin, facebook etc
- Want to build a following of subscribers who like their content

P3 can be used to create, maintain, and publish any type of information for any domain of interest:

- ♦ Best Practice
    - ♦ Management
    - ♦ Enterprise Architecture
    - ♦ Drilling oil wells
    - ♦ Banking
    - ♦ Pharma…
- ♦ Sales play books
- ♦ Stories

The content can be structured around any domains you like, although P3 provides 5 fundamental MAGIC domains for grouping best practice information:

- ♦ Methods - Methodologies
- ♦ Artefacts - Ontologies
- ♦ Guidance – Principles, policies, Standards…
- ♦ Items - Technologies
- ♦ Culture - Ethics, Values, Roles…

It provides a consistent updated taxonomy of knowledge that can be shared across all outputs and to all of the people (customers) using the content that it creates and manages.

Competitors

Before P3 was written, I spent some time looking for a component based publishing platform. At that time I discovered AuthorIT https://www.author-it.com/ but after spending some time to review it by actively use it, it became obvious that it could not meet my needs.

Introduction

Introduction

> ### KEYPOINT:
>
> P3 is a component based authoring system.

> ### ADOPTION:
>
> Management: Adopt the Pragmatic Publishing Platform to streamline your Pragmatic X-Framework adoption.

Questions to Ponder

- ◆ What do you currently use to maintain and publish the frameworks your Enterprise uses?
- ◆ What other uses can you think of for the Pragmatic Publishing Platform?

Frameworks

```
KEYPOINT:

The Frameworks section of PF2

introduces the Frameworks that are

part of the Pragmatic Family.
```

Questions to Ponder

- ◆ Do you think fundamental terminology is useful to your Enterprise?
- ◆ What fundamental terminology does your Enterprise use?
- ◆ If none, what fundamental terminology do you think would be appropriate?

Frameworks

In common with all Frameworks and Ontologies there are many good places to start, but no single "right place". Most things are connected and related to other things in some way and many dependencies exist whereby to understand one thing you need to have first understood a previous thing, but this thing may also require something previous to have been understood. After a while, circular dependencies become commonplace. To understand it all, you need to have first understood it all!

One approach is to read it sequentially: PF2 Introduction, PEFF, POET then PEAF and while every attempt has been made to ensure that creates a good learning environment and progression.

Another way is to think of it projected on a sphere with its content spread all over the surface where there is no single place to start and no single way of navigating through it. Different people will require different starting points and different people will have "aha!" moments at different times for different reasons.

However, there are two basic approaches. Which is best for you (or a merging of the two) is down to the individual reader:

- ◆ The first is to effectively just use it as a reference work and dip into things that look applicable as you go through your daily life and work.
- ◆ The second is to adopt a more systematic approach and just start at the beginning and keep reading until you are done!

Whichever way you choose, it should be taken into account that reading and learning something multiple times is the best way. We all learn by associating new information to what we already know - our context. Each time you read and learn, your previous learning provides more context for more learning. This builds and builds until the subject becomes part of your context. When that happens, the information has been fully learned and understood.

In the same way that the impact from the Death Star in Star Wars could not be fully realised unless the whole thing worked, so **Pragmatic**'s Ontologies and Frameworks will not be fully understood unless the whole is understood.

Of course, it is anticipated that **Pragmatic**'s Ontologies and Frameworks are used solely for positive rather than nefarious purposes, but like all tools (**Pragmatic**'s Ontologies and Frameworks are tools for the mind) if used incorrectly, they can be extremely dangerous! Not only for the person utilising it, but also for all those in the immediate vicinity!

> # KEYPOINT:
>
> To understand the whole, you first must understand the whole.

> # ADOPTION:
>
> EA Project Team: Repeat training and reading to fully understand the Frameworks and how to adopt them.

Questions to Ponder

- How many times will you read this book?
- How will you read this book? From cover to cover? Dipping into sections on as needed basis?
- Following the approach shown above?
- Will you go on a training course?

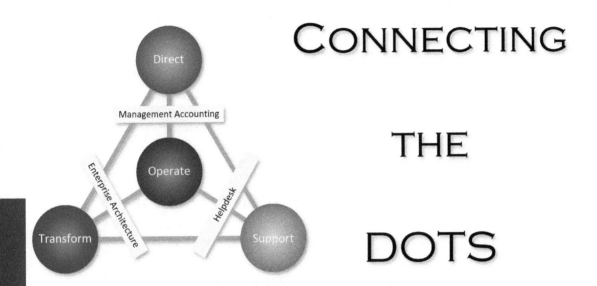

CONNECTING

THE

DOTS

The **Pragmatic** Family of Frameworks (**PF2**)is all about **Connecting the DOTS**™, but what does that actually mean? The aim is to make sure we understand the fundamental parts of the Enterprise, but more importantly to understand how those parts link together - as one coherent, cooperating set of MAGIC (Methods, Artefacts, Guidance, Items and Culture) to enable the Enterprise to achieve its objectives in an effective, efficient, agile and sustainable way.

For until we **understand how they can link together** as one coherent cooperating set of MAGIC, we will not be able to **mature how they can link together.** While there are many things that one could postulate that connect these parts, we illustrate here our view.

Enterprise Architecture - Decision Support for Transformation in relation to Operation, Direction and Support. We say that Enterprise Architecture is the glue that connects the Transformation domain to all the others because Enterprise Architecture is Transformation focussed and is the decision support tool used to plan the execution and transformation of Transformation.

Management Accounting - Decision Support for Direction in relation to Operation, Transformation and Support. We say that Management Accounting is the glue that connects the Direction domain to all the others because Management Accounting is Direction focussed and is the decision support tool used to plan the execution and transformation of Direction.

Helpdesk - Decision Support for Support in relation to Operation, Direction & Transformation. Hmmm, here we are not sure. Does this mean that our model is broken? Maybe. But it does not prove it is broken. For example, Management Accounting did not appear in this model until I understood what Management Accounting was. Until that time, that part of the model was empty too. So what is the missing part for Support?

KEYPOINT:

The Pragmatic Family of Frameworks
are all about Connecting the
DOTS™.

Questions to Ponder

♦ Do you agree with the placement of Enterprise Architecture and Management Accounting?

♦ What discipline would you suggest to replace the question marks?

The Pragmatic Family of Frameworks

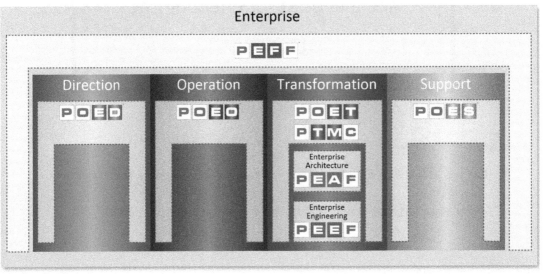

© Pragmatic 365 (2008-2021)

PF2 consists of a coherent and holistic set of Ontologies and Frameworks, that are designed to help improve the maturity of how Enterprises carry out their business in the four strategically important areas as defined by DOTS – Direction, Operation, Transformation and Support.

Each Framework is designed to be:

Pragmatic	Provide 80% of the benefits for only 20% of the effort.
Well-defined	Deal with a well-defined domain.
Complete	Be complete in scope with no overlaps and no gaps (not the same as complete in terms of detail. Detail is provided by Frameworks to the right).
Interlocking	Connect to and interface with frameworks at the same level.
Inheritable	Each framework inherits and builds on the content and guidance from Frameworks to the left and provides content and guidance to frameworks to the right.
Extensible	Helps Enterprises create their own frameworks by inheriting as much or as little as they deem appropriate from whatever level they deem appropriate.

PEFF is the **Pragmatic** <u>**Enterprise Fundamentals**</u> **Framework.** It sets out a set of universal ontologies and guidance that applies to all parts of an Enterprise. All other Frameworks inherit from PEFF.

♦ **POED** - The **Pragmatic** Operating model for <u>Enterprise Direction</u> sets the context for the Direction part of the Enterprise. It defines the MAGIC and things, that apply to all parts of Direction, that serve to set the context to increase the maturity of its individual parts.

♦ **POEO** - The **Pragmatic** Operating model for <u>Enterprise Operation</u> sets the context for the Operations part of the Enterprise. It defines the MAGIC, that apply to all parts of Operations, that serve to set the context to increase the maturity of its individual parts.

♦ **POET** - The **Pragmatic** Operating model for <u>Enterprise Transformation</u> sets the context for the Transformation part of the Enterprise. It defines the MAGIC, that apply to all parts of Transformation, that serve to set the context to increase the maturity of its individual parts (Strategising, Roadmapping, Solutioning, Elaboration, Construction and Transitioning and Governance).

♦ **POES** - The **Pragmatic** Operating model for <u>Enterprise Support</u> sets the context for the Support part of the Enterprise. It defines the MAGIC, that apply to all parts of Support, that serve to set the context to increase the maturity of its individual parts.

♦ **PTMC** - The **Pragmatic** <u>Transformation Maturity</u> Canvas provides a high level set of categories (a Canvas) for gathering feedback (Strengths, Weaknesses, Opportunities, Threats) regarding an Enterprise's Transformation Capability (from those who work within it) and for evaluating its maturity.

In the Transformation domain, POET provides the context for two further frameworks.

♦ **PEAF** - The **Pragmatic** <u>Enterprise Architecture</u> Framework sets the context for the Roadmapping part of Transformation (Enterprise Architecture). It defines the MAGIC (Methods, Artefacts, Guidance, Items and Cultural things) that serve to set the context to increase their maturity. PEAF is based on and inherits from POET and therefore POET is a pre-requisite for understanding and adopting PEAF.

♦ **PEEF** - The **Pragmatic** <u>Enterprise Engineering</u> Framework sets the context for the Solutioning, Elaboration, Construction and Transitioning parts of Transformation (Enterprise Engineering). It defines the MAGIC (Methods, Artefacts, Guidance, Items and Cultural things) that serve to set the context to increase their maturity. PEEF is based on and inherits from POET and therefore POET is a pre-requisite for understanding and adopting PEEF.

It is important to re-iterate that the relationships between the higher level frameworks and lower levels ones, are not one of decomposition, but are one of inheritance. Therefore, to adopt any lower level framework, the ontology that it inherits from must be understood first. For example, in order to understand and adopt PEAF or PEEF, it is a pre-requisite for POET be understood first.

Frameworks

> # KEYPOINT:
>
> Pragmatic Frameworks are Pragmatic,
>
> Well-defined, Complete, Interlocking,
>
> Inheritable and Extensible.

Questions to Ponder

♦ Do you know of other frameworks that could replace POED, POEO, POET and POES?

♦ How would you place frameworks you know on this diagram?

♦ Do you know of any frameworks that do not fit anywhere on this diagram?

Frameworks

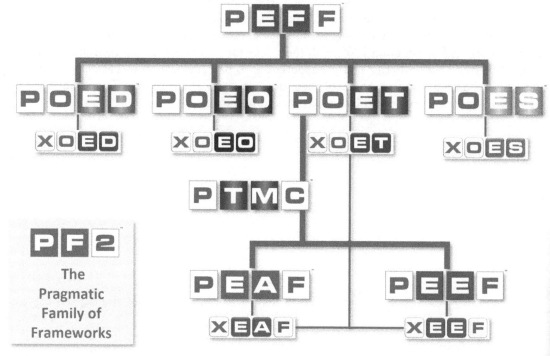

© Pragmatic 365 (2008-2021)

Any framework will never be 100% correct for 100% of Enterprises. Therefore, it is reasonable for users of frameworks to view them in terms of adopting and levering what works for them. This is generally accepted. The question is, how?

The X-Frameworks and Ontologies illustrate the way an Enterprise can use **Pragmatic**'s Frameworks as a basis to create their own Enterprise specific (X) frameworks by taking a **Pragmatic** Framework (or Ontology) and making the necessary changes required, in terms of content, branding, naming etc. The "X" is used as a placeholder that is meant to be replaced by an acronym specific to your Enterprise.

Most other frameworks only provide the absolute minimum help (generally nothing!) to adopt them for two main reasons:

♦ **Tailoring** - Firstly, in terms of being able to tailor a framework to your Enterprise so that it becomes your framework. This is usually because framework providers do not want to give you their "crown jewels". Doing so would enable you as an End-User Organisation to do a lot of the work yourself, without the need to spend large amounts of money on external consultants to do so.

♦ **Adoption** - Secondly, in terms of levels of maturity and how to go about adopting the framework. Again, this is usually because framework providers do not want to give Enterprises those things because if they did then those Enterprise could adopt them with much less "help" from outside consultancies.

Pragmatic takes a distinctly different view by being committed to providing as much collateral and guidance as possible, in order to keep the money spent on external consultants (including our own!) to a minimum, in addition to reducing the risk of failure.

The **Pragmatic** way for an Enterprise to adopt any framework (and thereby increase its maturity in a particular domain) is for that Enterprise to do so themselves (perhaps supported by an external consultant operating in a supporting, mentoring and facilitating role) rather than something a consultancy comes in and does "to you".

We absolutely understand that most of the time peoples "day jobs" do not allow them to spend time modifying and adopting a framework, but we believe that rather than allowing your existing staff to continue 100% with their "day job" and then paying consultants to come in and "do it to you", a better use of resources is to pay consultants to backfill your existing people (if required), to free some of their time to allow them to modify and adopting the framework (possibly supported by an external consultant).

> ## KEYPOINT:
>
> Pragmatic Frameworks were
>
> designed to be modified.

> ## ADOPTION:
>
> EA Project Team: Modify POET and
>
> PEAF as necessary (0-10%) to
>
> produce the Enterprise specific
>
> XOET and xEAF.

Questions to Ponder

- What Frameworks have you adopted (or tried to adopt) in the past?
- How easy was it?
- How much help and guidance was provided "out of the box"?
- How easy was it to modify and augment the framework?
- How much consultancy time and money was required?
- Was the adoption successful?

 The Pragmatic Family of Frameworks

Applicable to the whole Enterprise	Applicable to the Enterprise's Transformation Capability	Apllicable to the Enterprise's Enterprise Architecture Capability	Applicable to the Enterprise's Enterprise Engineering Capability
PEFF	PEFF	PEFF	PEFF
	POET	POET	POET
		PEAF	PEEF

© Pragmatic 365 (2008-2021)

Pragmatic's Frameworks are object oriented in nature, therefore each lower level framework extends (sub-classes) the higher level framework.

So, while PEFF covers topics that apply to the whole Enterprise, those topics apply equally to the Transformation Capability and the Enterprise Architecture Capability. Similarly, while POET covers topics that apply to the Transformation Capability, those topics apply equally to the Enterprise Architecture and Engineering Capabilities.

An implication of this is, for study purposes it is advisable to study the content in the PEFF, POET, PEAF/PEEF order.

An alternative to studying PEFF then POET then PEAF, is to study using the 4 Certification training modules which covers all the same content, but has been organised in the most effective way to learn the content:

A misconception here for people who want to learn about EA, is thinking that you can skip PEFF and POET and go straight to PEAF. This is not the case.

PEFF applies to Enterprise Architecture. It's just that PEFF also applies to things that are not EA.

POET applies to Enterprise Architecture. It's just that POET also applies to things that are not EA.

KEYPOINT:

PEAF inherits from POET inherits from PF2.

ADOPTION:

All: First Study PF2. Second Study POET. Third study PEAF.

Questions to Ponder

- ◆ Which Frameworks do you know of, that are applicable to the Whole of an Enterprise?
- ◆ Which Frameworks do you know of, that are applicable to an Enterprise's Transformation Capability?
- ◆ Which Frameworks do you know of, that are applicable to an Enterprise's EA Capability?
- ◆ Which Frameworks does your Enterprise use, that are applicable to the Whole of the Enterprise?
- ◆ Which Frameworks does your Enterprise use, that are applicable to it's Transformation Capability?
- ◆ Which Frameworks does your Enterprise use, that are applicable to it's EA Capability?

Frameworks

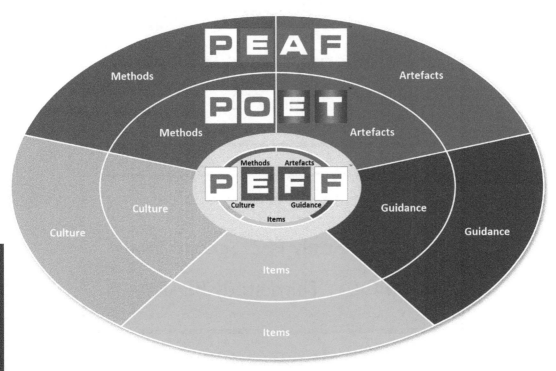

© Pragmatic 365 (2008-2021)

The relationships between the frameworks is important.

PEFF sits and the centre and defines the context and foundation for all other frameworks. One thing PEFF defines is MAGIC (Methods, Artefacts, Guidance, Items, Culture) which is a fundamentals structural ontology that all other frameworks are based upon.

POET is based up and extends PEFF into the Transformation domain. In this way, PEFF provides the context for POET.

PEAF is based up and extends POET into the Enterprise Architecture domain. In this way, POET provides the context for PEAF.

In this way, the all-important context for each framework is set by the frameworks that precede them.

Frameworks

KEYPOINT:

PEFF provides the Context for POET

provides the Context for PEAF.

ADOPTION:

EA Project Team: Make sure you

adopt all the frameworks that a

framework inherits from.

Questions to Ponder

- ♦ What frameworks does your Enterprise use?
- ♦ How are the frameworks you use, related?
- ♦ Is your Enterprise reaping the benefits that were anticipated?
- ♦ If not, why not?

Frameworks

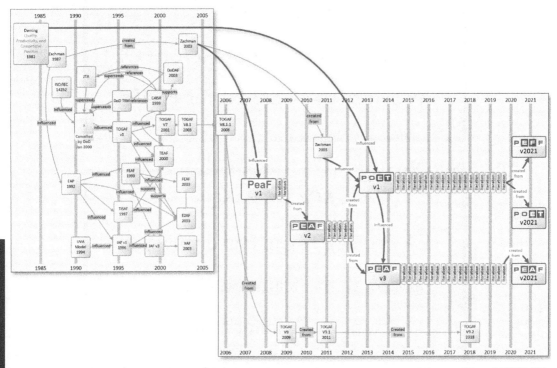

© Pragmatic 365 (2008-2021)

Businesses should concentrate on what they are good at. They should concentrate on their core business. Frameworks allow an Enterprise to do something without having to start from scratch. Frameworks should allow Enterprises to lever accepted wisdom without them having to invest huge amounts of time and money. But do they?

Here we see the timeline of many "EA Frameworks" and what influenced POET and PEAF.

All of these frameworks except PEAF are not true EA frameworks as they limit themselves to IT and the things that touch IT. They also tend to be more concerned with in project execution rather than cross project planning.

An important thing to note here is that PEAF (and subsequently POET and PEAF) have all developed through iteration. The live materials on the website and training is constantly evolving as new thinking is incorporated, and therefore new versions represent an accumulation of changes and improvements over time. This is in stark contrast to TOGAF that appears very much monolithic, with no incremental developments except large releases every 5 years or so.

> # KEYPOINT:
>
> Pragmatic Frameworks were mostly influenced by the thinking of Deming and Zachman.

Questions to Ponder

- ♦ What influenced the frameworks you use?
- ♦ Are there any influences that your Enterprise has ignored?

Frameworks

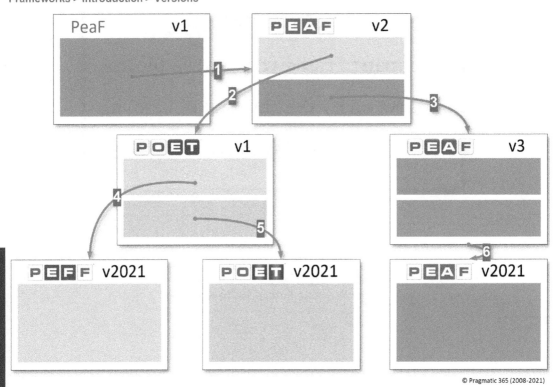

© Pragmatic 365 (2008-2021)

Frameworks

2008 PeaFv1

PEAF v1 was launched in November 2008 after many years of development. From a sea of EA noise and hype, PEAF "Cuts EA to the Bone" and provides a quick start toolkit necessary to setup and/or mature an Enterprise Architecture capability.

2010 PEAFv2

Over time, it became apparent that people were having trouble understanding EA because they did not know where EA fitted into the wider picture.

For this reason, PEAF v2 was born where a lot more contextual guidance was added.

2013 POETv1, PEAFv3

Over time, it became apparent that some things that PEAF contained, applied not only to the Enterprise Architecture domain but to the wider Enterprise Transformation domain.

For this reason, POET v1 was created and the things in PEAF that applied to the whole Enterprise Transformation domain were moved into POET. In addition, because POET now considered the wider Enterprise Transformation domain there were new things that were added to POET.

PEAF v3 was then created by taking the things from PEAF v2 that were purely concerned with the Enterprise Architecture domain, adding more things, and restructuring the content to conform to the new structures that POET had created.

2021 PEFFv2021, POETv2021, PEAF v2021

Over time, it became apparent that there were some parts of POET v1 that applied not only to the Transformation Domain of an Enterprise, but in fact to all parts of an Enterprise.

For this reason, PEFF v2021 was created, and the things in POET that applied to the whole Enterprise were moved into PEFF.

POET v2021 therefore became the remaining parts of POET v1 that were Transformation specific, but with a major reorganisation of the Adoption section and the expansion of MACE to MAGIC.

PEAF v2021 was mostly the same as PEAF v3, but with a major reorganisation of the Adoption section and the expansion of MACE to MAGIC.

The v2021 release also saw the harmonization of the versioning numbers and a change to the year of release.

It should be noted that none of this was pre-planned. PEFF, POET and PEAF have grown organically as time has passed. Had I tried to create PEFF POET and PEAF in 2008, I think I would have failed dismally.

A quote from Douglas Adams expresses it nicely:

> "I may not have gone where I intended to go, but I think I have ended up where I needed to be."
>
> *- Douglas Adams, The Long Dark Tea-Time of the Soul*

> # KEYPOINT:
>
> POET grew out of things originally in PEAF, that applied to all of the Transformation space, not just the EA part.

Questions to Ponder

♦ Did you know PEAF v2?
♦ Do you know the difference in domain, between POET and PEAF?

Frameworks

Frameworks > Available Now > PEFF (Enterprise Fundamentals)

Enterprise Fundamentals

Most things in the world today are hopelessly fragmented, and things that are supposed to bring things together, seem to be doing the exact opposite.

Why is this the case?

I believe it is because, in general, most people ache for more detail, more and more depth. Because getting into more and more detail, and more and more depth is comforting. More and more detail and more and more depth, make people experts in a particular field. It is a route to career development (more responsibility and more money) whilst still staying in your comfort zone.

There is nothing inherently wrong with this per se. It is how experts are born. But, for everyone to be able to operate in their own comfort zone, and for various comfort zones to work together harmoniously we must look at the bigger picture - and therein lies the problem. The bigger picture takes people out of their comfort zone.

Foundations are important. Everyone knows that. No one would build a house without good foundations, and no one would buy a house without good foundations. But that is only physical foundations.

Foundations also exist in knowledge about things, and approaches to achieving things, but the world has become obsessed with more and more depth and more and more detail.

It seems to be acceptable nowadays to treat with derision, anyone that even remotely comes close, to talking about something that is not buried in vast amounts of detail. It appears to have become accepted, that advancement comes with just creating more detail, rather than considering things from a more fundamental perspective.

So although everyone knows that foundations are important, why is it that no one seems to be in the least bit interested in them?

Detail has brought us far, but is more and more detail going to get us to where we want to be? Need to be? Of course there will always be detail, but is detail enough in the 21st Century?

The more people and Enterprises have concentrated on detail, the more detached they have become from important fundamentals.

PEFF sets out some fundamental definitions and ontologies that are used by all other frameworks in the family.

KEYPOINT:

PEFF - The Pragmatic Enterprise Fundamentals Framework.

ADOPTION:

C-Suite: Instigate a review of the Enterprise's EA Capability, and determine if PEFF can be useful to the Enterprise.

Questions to Ponder

- ◆ How do Enterprise Architecture frameworks that you know of, compare to PEAF?

PEFF allows Executive Management to take a coherent and holistic **view** of their **Whole Enterprise,**

by providing **fundamental structures**, to enable **informed decision making,**

allowing them to pragmatically increase its **Effectiveness and Efficiency.**

KEYPOINT:

PEEF allows an Enterprise to define

and put in place fundamental

Ontologies used throughout an

Enterprise.

ADOPTION:

Management: Use PEFF to instill a set

of fundamental strategically important

Ontologies into the Enterprise.

Questions to Ponder

- ♦ Do you think holistic and coherents Ontoliges is beneficial to your Enterprise?
- ♦ How much time and money does your Enterprise spend on Fundamentals?

Enterprise Transformation

"The only constant is change!" has been the battle cry for many years but just being able to deal with change is no longer enough. The new battle cry is "The only constant is the acceleration of change!"

How an Enterprise effects the whole of Transformation is becoming a Strategic Strength or a Strategic Weakness, where massive business opportunities can be gained or massive business problems will result.

POET (by providing a framework) allows those involved in the Transformation of Enterprises (from the "Chief Transformation Officer" to those physically deploying the changes, and all those in between) to take a coherent and holistic view of the MAGIC of the Transformation part of an Enterprise (from Strategy to Deployment) to allow Executive Management (by enabling informed decisions) to improve it

Not the Transformation of Operations, but the Transformation of Transformation, to better enable the Transformation of Operations.

KEYPOINT:

POET - The Pragmatic Operating model for Enterprise Transformation.

ADOPTION:

C-Suite: Instigate a review of the Enterprise's Transformation Capability, and determine if POET can be useful to the Enterprise.

Questions to Ponder

♦ What frameworks that you know of, fit into the Transformation domain?

Frameworks

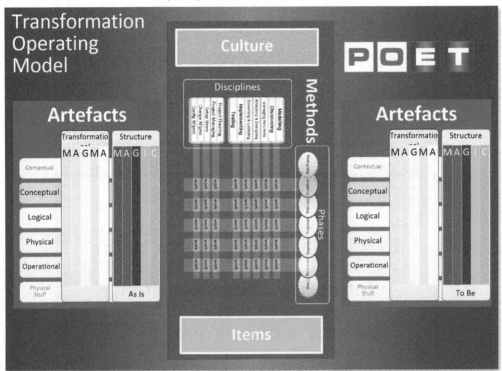

© Pragmatic 365 (2008-2021)

Here we see how the phases and disciplines involved in Transformation operate on the Structural and Transformational Artefacts. This is the domain that POET helps to structure. POET effectively defines the Conceptual Operating Model for Enterprise Transformation.

The structural Artefacts relate to the structure of the thing we are transforming - usually Operations.

Within your Enterprise, Transformation is using an Operating Model - whether it is good or bad, documented or not.

Frameworks

KEYPOINT:

POET allows you to Strategically guide the Tactical changes, to the Transformation capability of your Enterprise.

ADOPTION:

C-Suite: Mandate the use of POET to Strategically guide, Tactical changes to the Transformation capability of your Enterprise.

Questions to Ponder

♦ What Operating model do you use for Transformation?
♦ Do people know what it is?
♦ Is it fit for purpose?
♦ If not, who is Accountable for improving it?
♦ Who is Responsible for improving it?

Frameworks

POET allows Executive Management to take a coherent and holistic **view** of their **Transformation Capability**,

by providing a coherent & holistic MAGIC Framework, to enable **informed decision making**,

allowing them to pragmatically increase its **Effectiveness and Efficiency.**

© Pragmatic 365 (2008-2021)

KEYPOINT:

POET allows an Enterprise to take a coherent and holistic view of the Transformation part of your Enterprise.

ADOPTION:

Management: Use POET to take a coherent and holistic view of the Transformation part of your Enterprise.

Questions to Ponder

♦ Do you think a holistic and coherent framework for Enterprise Transformation is beneficial?

♦ How much time and money does your Enterprise spend on Transformation?

♦ How much time and money does your Enterprise spend on transforming HOW they effect Transformation?

Frameworks

An Operating Model
for Transformation

which allows you to...
Think Strategically

which allows you to...
Act Tactically

© Pragmatic 365 (2008-2021)

POET effectively defines an Operating Model for the Enterprise Transformation domain. As such, POET should be used in the same way as any other Operating Model - a means to organise and orchestrate all the parts together into a coherent whole, whose focus is the end to end efficiency and effectiveness of the whole domain, not the efficiency or effectiveness of only its parts.

An Operating Model does not tell people exactly what to do, when, how and with what. If it did, it would not be an Operating Model and it would not fulfil its purpose.

POET does not tell you what frameworks to use to improve the Transformation domain. It does not matter if an Enterprise wishes to use PEAF, ITIL, MSP, TOGAF, COBIT, RUP, MoV or any of hundreds of frameworks that currently exist. What does matter is that an Enterprise adopts the frameworks they select within the holistic and coherent context that POET provides.

"How should I use POET?" is a common and perfectly reasonable question. However, it can be closely followed by …

> "It's too big - I can't tell someone we are going to improve the MAGIC of everyone and everything related to Transformation - it's just too big! No one is going to go for that!"

Which incorrectly implies that we are advocating that there should be a massive project to improve the whole of the Transformation domain in one fell swoop. We are not. Whilst POET encompasses the entire Transformation domain (from Strategy to Deployment) this does not mean that an Enterprise should embark on improving the entire Transformation domain in one fell swoop.

Tactical and piecemeal changes to parts of the Transformation domain is a perfectly reasonable way to improve things (evolution no revolution) **but these changes need to be made in the context of a wider plan and an understanding of how the part that is being changed, relates to the larger and more important whole.**

Most Enterprises do make some (not enough) changes to **How** they effect Transformation. Maybe they adopt ITIL or COBIT or PRINCE2. Maybe they buy some software tools to help manage the risks or requirements. There is nothing wrong with that per se. What is wrong, and where many problems come from, is that they do so without a clear understanding of how the part they are changing is related to other parts of the Transformation domain.

POET allows Enterprises to think strategically so they can then act tactically with respect to the Transformation domain instead of just acting tactically.

But the people in Enterprises can only think strategically if they are given **time to think**. If an Enterprise constantly drives its people to act and discourages them from doing anything else (because if you are not acting then you are not working) then they will be acting tactically without thinking strategically. This means that you will almost certainly win the battle. It also means that you will almost certainly lose the war.

So, a Logical model for Enterprise Architecture is needed to allow you to think Strategically.

And you need to think Strategically, to be able to act Tactically.

Acting Tactically without any Strategic plan is often referred to as, being a "loose cannon".

> "Strategy without tactics is the slowest route to victory.
> Tactics without strategy is the noise before defeat"
>
> *- Sun Tzu*

> "Strategy without tactics is the slowest route to victory.
> Tactics without strategy is the fastest route to defeat"
>
> **- Pragmatic**

Frameworks

KEYPOINT:

POET allows an Enterprise to Tactically improve parts of Transformation, in the context of the Strategic whole.

ADOPTION:

Management: Use POET to enable Tactically improve parts of Transformation, in the context of the Strategic whole.

Questions to Ponder

◆ What Operating Model for Transformation does your Enterprise use?

◆ If it doesn't use one, does that cause any problems?

◆ Does your Enterprise think strategically and act tactically or just act tactically (with respect to improving How it effects Transformation)?

◆ What initiatives has your Enterprise undertaken to improve How Transformation is effected?

◆ What did your Enterprise use to ensure that those initiatives fitted into a holistic and coherent strategy?

Enterprise Architecture

In many respects Enterprise Architecture can be compared to gardening - or more accurately the MAGIC that allow a gardener to produce a pleasant garden or to grow fruit and vegetables.

A lot of people try to "sell" Enterprise Architecture with quick wins and low-hanging fruit. Whilst we will certainly not ignore such opportunities if they exist, to pursue only those quick wins is totally against the raison d'être of Enterprise Architecture.

Enterprise Architecture is concerned with creating the correct environment for the gardener and the garden to be effective and efficient. Creating the correct environment does not in itself create the garden, but as every gardener will know, that environment can have a massive positive or negative impact on the garden. This is exactly the same for Enterprise Architecture - we are creating the environment required for an Enterprise (participating in an Enterprise) to grow, to flourish, to bloom and to bear fruit - not only for this year but for next year and for many years to come. Implementing changes to become more mature in how Enterprise Architecture is utilised does not in itself do this, but provides the environment for this to happen.

Many gardeners also know you can try to create the correct environment through trial and error (and sometimes for specific reasons it is beneficial to do this), but generally speaking the best gardeners lever and utilise the tips, tricks and knowledge of other gardeners as much as possible. In this respect, they are using Frameworks.

There is a lot information about Enterprise Architecture. Much of it is conflicting, inconsistent, inapplicable or unusable. This is why PEAF was created - to provide a small and concise set of real things to use rather than long winded ivory tower opinion and explanations - knowledge that will allow the garden and the gardener to flourish.

Kevin Lee Smith

*The **Pragmatic** Gardener*

Frameworks

Frameworks

KEYPOINT:

PEAF - The Pragmatic Enterprise Architecture Framework.

ADOPTION:

C-Suite: Instigate a review of the Enterprise's EA Capability, and determine if PEAF can be useful to the Enterprise.

Questions to Ponder

♦ How do Enterprise Architecture frameworks that you know of, compare to PEAF?

Frameworks

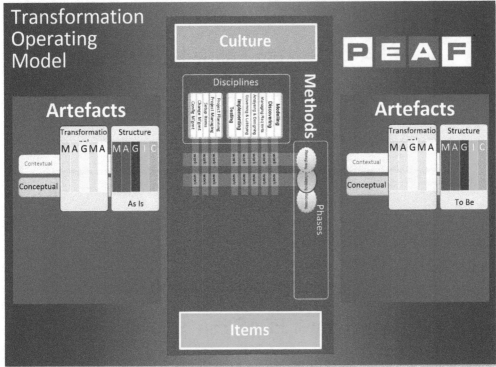

© Pragmatic 365 (2008-2021)

Here we see how the phases and disciplines involved in Enterprise Architecture operate on the Structural and Transformational Artefacts. This is the domain that PEAF helps to structure. PEAF effectively defines the Logical Model for Enterprise Architecture.

The structural Artefacts relate to the structure of the thing we are transforming - usually Operations.

Within your Enterprise, Transformation is using Enterprise Architecture - whether it is good or bad, documented or not.

> # KEYPOINT:
>
> POET allows you to Strategically guide the Tactical changes, to the Transformation capability of your Enterprise.

> # ADOPTION:
>
> C-Suite: Mandate the use of POET to Strategically guide, Tactical changes to the Transformation capability of your Enterprise.

Questions to Ponder

- ♦ What Operating model do you use for Transformation?
- ♦ Do people know what it is?
- ♦ Is it fit for purpose?
- ♦ If not, who is Accountable for improving it?
- ♦ Who is Responsible for improving it?

PEAF allows Executive Management to take a coherent and holistic **view** of their **Enterprise Architecture Capability**,

by providing a coherent & holistic MAGIC Framework, to enable **informed decision making**,

allowing them to pragmatically increase its **Effectiveness and Efficiency.**

KEYPOINT:

PEAF allows an Enterprise to take a coherent and holistic view of the Strategising and Roadmapping (EA) Transformation phases of your Enterprise.

ADOPTION:

Management: Use PEAF to take a coherent and holistic view of the Transformation part of your Enterprise.

Questions to Ponder

- ◆ Do you think a holistic and coherent framework for Enterprise Architecture is beneficial?
- ◆ How much time and money does your Enterprise spend on Strategising and Roadmapping?
- ◆ How much time and money does your Enterprise spend on transforming HOW it executes Strategising and Roadmapping?

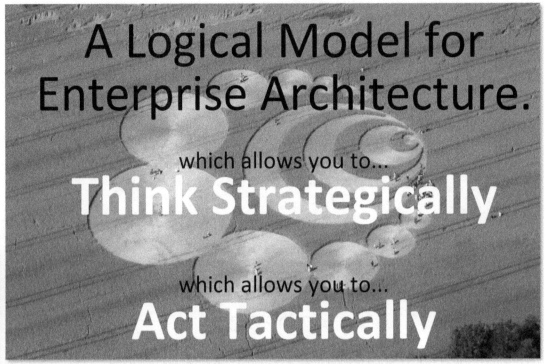

A Logical Model for Enterprise Architecture.

which allows you to...

Think Strategically

which allows you to...

Act Tactically

© Pragmatic 365 (2008-2021)

Frameworks

PEAF effectively defines a Logical Model for the Enterprise Architecture domain. As such, PEAF should be used in the same way as any other Logical Model - a means to organise and orchestrate all the physical parts of the EA capability in an Enterprise together, into a coherent whole, whose focus is the end to end efficiency and effectiveness of the whole domain, not the efficiency or effectiveness of only its parts.

A Logical Model does not tell people exactly what to do, when, how and with what. If it did, it would not be an Logical Model and it would not fulfil its purpose.

"How should I use PEAF?" is a common and perfectly reasonable question. However, it can be closely followed by …

> "It's too big - I can't tell someone we are going to improve the Methods,
> Artefacts, Guidance, Items and Culture of everyone and everything related
> to Transformation - it's just too big! No one is going to go for that!"

Which incorrectly implies that we are advocating that there should be a massive project to improve the whole of the EA domain in one fell swoop. We are not. Whilst PEAF encompasses the entire EA domain (Strategising, Roadmapping and Project Governance) this does not mean that an Enterprise should embark on improving the entire EA domain in one fell swoop.

Tactical and piecemeal changes to parts of the EA domain is a way to improve things (evolution no revolution) **but these changes need to be made in the context of a wider plan and an understanding of how the part that is being changed, relates to the larger and more important whole.**

Most Enterprises do make some (not enough) changes to How they "do" EA. Maybe they create some principles. Maybe they buy an EA modelling Tool. There is nothing wrong with that per se. What is wrong, and where many problems come from, is that they do so without a clear understanding of how the part they are changing is related to other parts of the EA domain. It is akin to travelling without any clear idea of where your ultimate destination.

PEAF allows Enterprises to think strategically so they can then act tactically with respect to increasing the maturity of the Enterprise Architecture domain instead of just acting tactically.

But the people in Enterprises can only think strategically if they are given **time to think**. If an Enterprise constantly drives its people to act and discourages them from doing anything else (because if you are not acting then you are not working) then they will be acting tactically without thinking strategically. This means that you will almost certainly win the battle. It also means that you will almost certainly lose the war.

So, a Logical model for Enterprise Architecture is needed to allow you to think Strategically.

And you need to think Strategically, to be able to act Tactically.

Acting Tactically without any Strategic plan is often referred to as, being a "loose cannon".

> "Strategy without tactics is the slowest route to victory.
> Tactics without strategy is the **noise** before defeat"
>
> *- Sun Tzu*

> "Strategy without tactics is the slowest route to victory.
> Tactics without strategy is the **fastest route to** defeat"
>
> **- Pragmatic**

> # KEYPOINT:
>
> PEAF allows an Enterprise to Tactically improve parts of EA, in the context of the Strategic whole.

> # ADOPTION:
>
> Management: Use PEAF to enable Tactically improve parts of Transformation, in the context of the Strategic whole.

Questions to Ponder

- ◆ What Logical Model for Enterprise Architecture does your Enterprise use?
- ◆ If it doesn't use one, do you think it would be beneficial if it did?
- ◆ Does your Enterprise think strategically and act tactically or just act tactically (with respect to improving How it "does" EA)?
- ◆ What initiatives has your Enterprise undertaken to improve How EA is effected?
- ◆ What did your Enterprise use to ensure that those initiatives fitted into a holistic and coherent strategy?

TM

Transformation Maturity

KEYPOINT:

PTMC - The Pragmatic

Transformation Maturity Canvas.

ADOPTION:

Management: Use the PTMC to

pragmatically expose the good the

bad and the ugly with respect to your

Transformation domain.

Questions to Ponder

- ◆ How do Enterprise Transformation Maturity Canvasses that you know of, compare to PTMC?

PTMC allows Executive Management to **assess** the fitness of their **Transformation Capability**,

by providing a coherent & holistic MAGIC Framework, to enable **informed decision making**,

allowing them to pragmatically decide which parts to **tactically adjust**.

Frameworks

> ## KEYPOINT:
>
> PTMC allows an Enterprise to assess the fitness of the Transformation Capability of your Enterprise.

> ## ADOPTION:
>
> Management: Use the PTMC to assess the fitness of the Transformation Capability of your Enterprise.

Questions to Ponder

- ◆ Do you think a holistic and coherent framework for Enterprise Architecture is beneficial?
- ◆ How much time and money does your Enterprise spend on Strategising and Roadmapping?
- ◆ How much time and money does your Enterprise spend on transforming HOW it executes Strategising and Roadmapping?

An Assessment Tool for Enterprise Transformation.

which allows you to...
Think Strategically

which allows you to...
Act Tactically

© Pragmatic 365 (2008-2021)

The PTMC is an assessment tool for an Enterprise to be able to assess its Transformation Capability.

Many Enterprises do not take such an overall view and as such, tend to change parts of their Transformation Capability without understanding how the part they are changing fits into the whole Transformation Capability. And let's not forget, that it is the whole end to end Transformation Capability that is important to the C-Suite, not its parts. This usually results in one part being improved with little overall effect on improvement. This tends to be because the part feeding the part that was improved, is not of sufficient quality, or because the part that receives the output of the part that was improved, is not of sufficient quality.

This allows you to think Strategically.

And you need to think Strategically, to be able to act Tactically.

Acting Tactically without any Strategic plan is often referred to as, being a "loose cannon".

> "Strategy without tactics is the slowest route to victory.
> Tactics without strategy is the **noise** before defeat"
>
> *- Sun Tzu*

> "Strategy without tactics is the slowest route to victory.
> Tactics without strategy is the **fastest route to** defeat"
>
> **- Pragmatic**

Frameworks

> # KEYPOINT:
>
> The PTMC allows an Enterprise to Strategically assess its Transformation Capability, so it can Tactically mature it.

> # ADOPTION:
>
> Management: Use the PTMC to Strategically assess its Transformation Capability.

Questions to Ponder

♦ What Logical Model for Enterprise Architecture does your Enterprise use?

♦ If it doesn't use one, do you think it would be beneficial if it did?

♦ Does your Enterprise think strategically and act tactically or just act tactically (with respect to improving How it "does" EA)?

♦ What initiatives has your Enterprise undertaken to improve How EA is effected?

♦ What did your Enterprise use to ensure that those initiatives fitted into a holistic and coherent strategy?

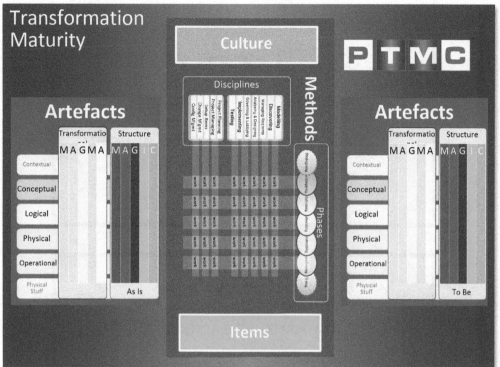

© Pragmatic 365 (2008-2021)

Here we see an identical map to that shown for POET.

The PTMC covers all the areas that POET covers, but the PTMC is only concerned with exposing the Strengths, Weaknesses, Opportunities and Threats of domain. In this way, it is part of POET.

KEYPOINT:

The PTMC allows you to

Pragmatically assess the

Transformation capability of your

Enterprise.

ADOPTION:

C-Suite: Mandate the use of PTMC to

assess the Transformation capability

of your Enterprise.

Questions to Ponder

♦ What assessment cavas do you use to assess your Transformation capability?
♦ Do people know what it is?
♦ Is it fit for purpose?
♦ If not, who is Accountable for improving it?
♦ Who is Responsible for improving it?

POED™

Enterprise

Direction

© Pragmatic 365 (2008-2021)

KEYPOINT:

POED - The Pragmatic Operating model for Enterprise Direction.

ADOPTION:

C-Suite: Instigate a review of the Enterprises Direction capability, and determine if POED can be useful to the Enterprise.

Questions to Ponder

♦ What frameworks that you know of, fit into the Direction domain?

Frameworks > Coming Soon > POED (Direction) > Overview

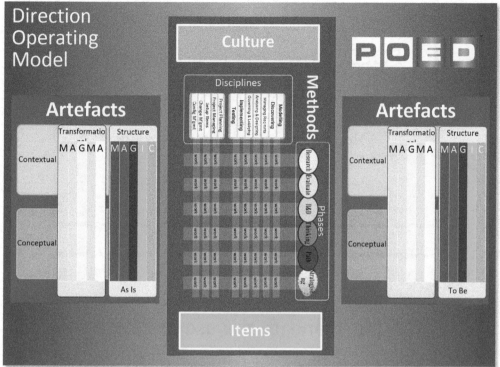

Direction is defined by MAGIC. This is the domain that POED helps to structure. POED effectively defines the Conceptual Operating Model for Enterprise Direction.

Within your Enterprise, Direction is using an Operating Model - whether it is good or bad, documented or not.

POED is currently under construction.

Frameworks

KEYPOINT:

POED allows you to Strategically guide the Tactical changes, to the Direction capability of your Enterprise.

ADOPTION:

C-Suite: Mandate the use of POED to Strategically guide, Tactical changes to the Direction capability of your Enterprise.

Questions to Ponder

- What Operating model do you use for Direction?
- Do people know what it is?
- Is it fit for purpose?
- If not, who is Accountable for improving it?
- Who is Responsible for improving it?

TM

Enterprise

Operation

> # KEYPOINT:
>
> POEO - The Pragmatic Operating model for Enterprise Operation.

> # ADOPTION:
>
> C-Suite: Instigate a review of the Enterprises Operation capability, and determine if **POEO** can be useful to the Enterprise.

Questions to Ponder

♦ What frameworks that you know of, fit into the Operation domain?

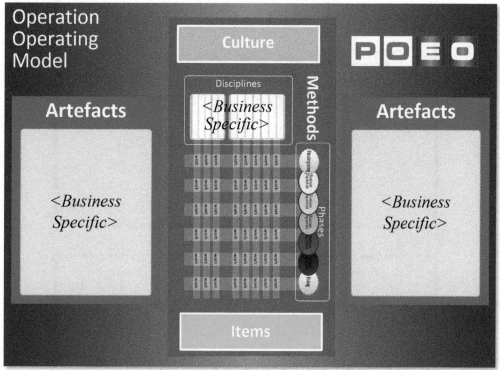

© Pragmatic 365 (2008-2021)

Operation is defined by MAGIC. The Phases, Disciplines and Artefacts are all Enterprise specific for each type of Enterprise - an Oil Company, a Health Agency, a University, an Aircraft Manufacturer, a Bank, etc. This is the domain that POEO helps to structure. POEO effectively defines the Conceptual Operating Model for Enterprise Operation.

Within your Enterprise, Operations is using an Operating Model - whether it is good or bad, documented or not.

POEO is currently under construction.

Frameworks

> # KEYPOINT:
>
> POEO allows you to Strategically guide the Tactical changes, to the Operation capability of your Enterprise.

> # ADOPTION:
>
> C-Suite: Mandate the use of POEO to Strategically guide, Tactical changes to the Operation capability of your Enterprise.

Questions to Ponder

- What Operating model do you use for Operations?
- Do people know what it is?
- Is it fit for purpose?
- If not, who is Accountable for improving it?
- Who is Responsible for improving it?

Frameworks

POES™

Enterprise
Support

KEYPOINT:

POES - The Pragmatic Operating model for Enterprise Support.

ADOPTION:

C-Suite: Instigate a review of the Enterprises Support capability, and determine if POES can be useful to the Enterprise.

Questions to Ponder

♦ What frameworks that you know of, fit into the Support domain?

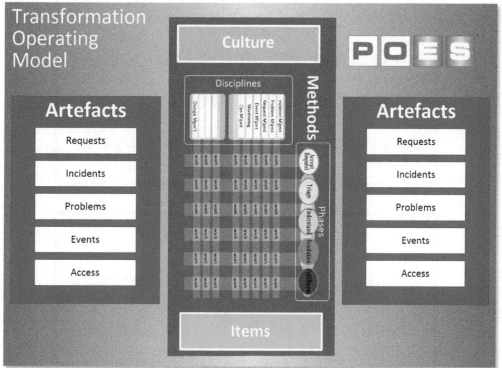

© Pragmatic 365 (2008-2021)

We can also see that Support is defined by MAGIC. The Phases, Disciplines and Artefacts are all related to Support. This is the domain that POES helps to structure. POES effectively defines the Conceptual Operating Model for Enterprise Support.

Within your Enterprise, Support is using an Operating Model - whether it is good or bad, documented or not.

POES is currently under construction.

> # KEYPOINT:
>
> POES allows you to Strategically guide the Tactical changes, to the Support capability of your Enterprise.

> # ADOPTION:
>
> C-Suite: Mandate the use of POES to Strategically guide, Tactical changes to the Support capability of your Enterprise.

Questions to Ponder

♦ What Operating model do you use for Support?
♦ Do people know what it is?
♦ Is it fit for purpose?
♦ If not, who is Accountable for improving it?
♦ Who is Responsible for improving it?
♦ Does your Support capability support many things or only IT?
♦ Do you have duplicate Support capabilities (first and second line) one for internal IT and one for customer's problems?
♦ If so, why?

PEEF ™

Enterprise Engineering

> # KEYPOINT:
>
> PEEF - The Pragmatic Enterprise Engineering Framework.

> # ADOPTION:
>
> C-Suite: Instigate a review of the Enterprise's Enterprise Engineering Capability, and determine if PEEF can be useful to the Enterprise.

Questions to Ponder

- How do Enterprise Engineering frameworks that you know of, compare to PEEF?

Frameworks > Coming Soon > PEEF (Enterprise Engineering) > Overview

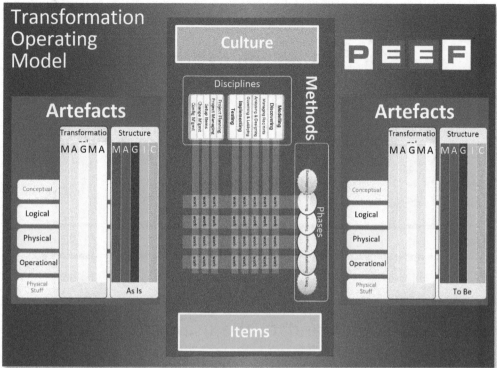

© Pragmatic 365 (2008-2021)

Here we see how the phases and disciplines involved in Enterprise Engineering operate on the Structural and Transformational Artefacts. This is the domain that PEEF helps to structure. PEEF effectively defines the Logical Model for Enterprise Engineering.

The structural Artefacts relate to the structure of the thing we are transforming - usually Operations.

Within your Enterprise, Transformation is using Enterprise Engineering - whether it is good or bad, documented or not.

KEYPOINT:

POET allows you to Strategically guide the Tactical changes, to the Transformation capability of your Enterprise.

ADOPTION:

C-Suite: Mandate the use of POET to Strategically guide, Tactical changes to the Transformation capability of your Enterprise.

Questions to Ponder

- ♦ What Operating model do you use for Transformation?
- ♦ Do people know what it is?
- ♦ Is it fit for purpose?
- ♦ If not, who is Accountable for improving it?
- ♦ Who is Responsible for improving it?

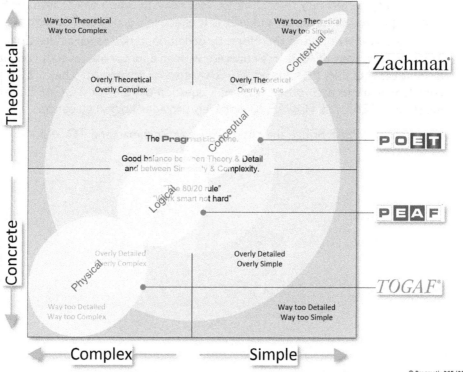

Way too Theoretical
Way too Complex

Way too Theoretical
Way too Simple

Zachman®

Overly Theoretical
Overly Complex

Overly Theoretical
Overly Simple

Contextual

POET

The Pragmatic one.

Good balance between Theory & Detail
and between Simplicity & Complexity.

Conceptual

PEAF

"The 80/20 rule"
"Work smart not hard"

Logical

Overly Detailed
Overly Complex

Overly Detailed
Overly Simple

TOGAF®

Physical

Way too Detailed
Way too Complex

Way too Detailed
Way too Simple

Theoretical — Concrete

Complex — Simple

© Pragmatic 365 (2008-2021)

Here we present a method of categorising frameworks and ontologies.

The vertical axis ranges between the Theoretical and the Concrete, while the horizontal axis ranges between the Simple and the Complex.

The green area illustrates a domain of balance between these extremes, where the 80/20 rule applies and a good balance between simplicity and complexity and between theory and concreteness is achieved.

The red area illustrates a range where these categorisations stray too far into extremes and the opposite of the 80/20 rule applies.

The blue area illustrates a range between these points.

- ◆ **Zachman** is an Ontology and is therefore Simple & Theoretical. However, it could be said that it is too Simple and too Theoretical to enable easy adoption. It effectively provides Contextual guidance.
- ◆ **TOGAF** is very Concrete and Complex. It could be said that it is too Concrete and too Complex to enable easy adoption. It effectively provides Physical guidance.

There is a noticeable chasm between them. Before POET and PEAF were created, many people found this chasm too wide to bridge. I have heard people who have attended Zachman training, come out and say "OK, that's was a nice grounding. What the hell do I do now!? Where do I start!?". Similarly, I have heard people who have attended TOGAF training, come out and say "OK, that's was a huge amount of stuff. What the hell do I do now!? Where do I start!?"

This chasm is what POET and PEAF were designed to fill.

- ◆ **POET** is an Ontology and therefore by definition tends towards the theoretical like Zachman. However, POET is less theoretical than Zachman with an appropriate level of complexity to make it easily usable. **Zachman and POET do not compete.** They are complementary to each other. It is not a question of Zachman or POET but more a question of Zachman and POET. It effectively provides Conceptual guidance.

♦ **PEAF** is a Framework and therefore, by definition, tends towards the Concrete like TOGAF. However, PEAF is less concrete with an appropriate level of complexity to make it easily usable. **PEAF and TOGAF do not compete.** They are complementary to each other. It is not a question of PEAF or TOGAF but more a question of PEAF and TOGAF. It effectively provides Logical guidance.

In this way, POET and PEAF bridge the chasm between Zachman and TOGAF.

KEYPOINT:

POET and PEAF bridge the chasm

between Zachman and TOGAF.

ADOPTION:

Management: Use POET and PEAF to

bridge the chasm between Zachman

and TOGAF.

Questions to Ponder

◆ Do you agree with this method of categorisation?
◆ If not, why not and how would you draw the diagram?
◆ Where would you place the Frameworks you currently use on this diagram?
◆ Where would you put Zachman?
◆ Where would you put TOGAF?
◆ Where would you put POET?
◆ Where would you put PEAF?
◆ How do other frameworks you use fit?
◆ What do you use to bridge the gaps between them?

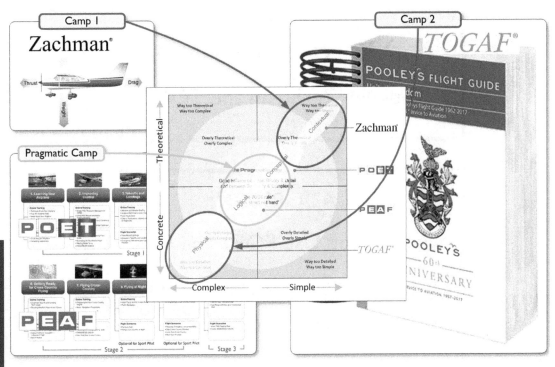

A common misunderstanding is that people misinterpret **Pragmatic**'s Frameworks in two totally opposing ways. Both of which cannot be correct.

People in Camp 1 say something like,

> "It's all a bit high level and conceptual to be adopted. It doesn't actually
> tell me what to do, and therefore, is of little practical use."

They view **Pragmatic**'s Frameworks as being as simplistic as a basic diagram on Aerodynamics is to a pilot.

People in Camp 2 say something like,

> "It's far too detailed and large to be adopted, will take too long to learn,
> will require massive change and therefore, is of little practical use."

They view **Pragmatic**'s Frameworks as being as complicated and complex as a full Flight manual is to a trainee pilot.

Plainly something is not right, as something cannot be too high level and conceptual and be too detailed and large at the same time. One of those camps must be wrong!

In fact, the truth is, they are both wrong.

But why do they think they are right? When someone who has not spent enough time understanding something, wishes to stop spending time understanding something, an easy get-out-of-jail-free card is to reject it, and an easy way to do that is to say that it's either too simple to be of any use, or its too complicated to be of any use. These people are not bad people. They are just "Slaves to Psychology™"

So, when people reject **Pragmatic**'s Frameworks, it is more to do with their understanding, which is a function of the time they have available, and the appetite they have for understanding them.

The reality is that **Pragmatic**'s Frameworks sit in a **Pragmatic** area between the two. They are more detailed than the simplistic views of Camp 1 and they are less detailed than the complex views of Camp 2.

To understand that **Pragmatic**'s Frameworks do not fit into Camp 1 or Camp2 we can refer back to the comparison of Zachman and TOGAF with POET and PEAF.

- ♦ Zachman is an example of a Framework that exists in Camp 1, because it is essentially just a grid and that's it.
- ♦ TOGAF is an example of a Framework that exists in Camp 2, because it is horrendously complicated, inconsistent and detailed.

It is precisely because of this, that POET and PEAF were written - to bridge that chasm.

Pragmatic's Frameworks, are in the **Pragmatic** Camp, were we provide more information and guidance than Camp 1 believes, and less detail and complexity than Camp 2 believes.

Perhaps people categorise **Pragmatic**'s Frameworks in these two camps because these two camps are the only camps they have ever known, and so they lump **Pragmatic**'s Frameworks into the same camp as the Frameworks that they already know aka Zachman and TOGAF. Frameworks that have frustrated them in the past, for either being too high level or too complicated.

Frameworks

> # KEYPOINT:
>
> People incorrectly think Pragmatic Frameworks are either too high level and conceptual or incorrectly think they are too large and detailed.

> # ADOPTION:
>
> EA Project Team: Use POET and PEAF in the way they were designed to be used.

Questions to Ponder

- Do you think Pragmatic Frameworks are a bit high level and conceptual to be adopted and therefore of little practical use?"
- Do you think Pragmatic Frameworks are far too detailed and large to be adopted and therefore of little practical use?"
- What time have you spent understanding them?
- What is your appetite to understand more?

Strategic	**Transformational Focus**
Project	How much the framework is focussed on Strategic Planning and Roadmapping vs Project Level work.
Enterprise	**Structural Focus**
IT	How much the framework is focussed on the structure of the entire Enterprise vs mostly IT.
Detail	**Content**
Usability	An indication of how detailed the framework is vs how usable it is.

Here we see some criteria that we will use to analyse and compare PEAF, TOGAF and Zachman:

Transformational Focus

♦ **Strategic** - Frameworks that score highly here are ones whose remit is more towards the Strategising, Roadmapping and governance of Solutioning phases of the Transformation domain - the domains typically associated with Enterprise Architecture.

♦ **Project** - Frameworks that score highly here are ones whose remit is more towards the Solutioning, Elaborating, and the governance of Construction phases of the Transformation domain - the domains typically associated with Enterprise Engineering.

Structural Focus

♦ **Enterprise** - Frameworks that score highly here are ones whose remit is more towards the structure of the entire Enterprise without limitation - the domain typically associated with Enterprise Architecture.

♦ **IT** - Frameworks that score highly here are ones whose remit is more towards the structure of only those parts of the Enterprise consisting of IT and the other parts of the Enterprise that are connected to IT in some way - the domain typically associated with Enterprise IT Architecture (EITA).

Content

♦ **Detail** - Frameworks that score highly here are ones that are large and contain massive amounts of detail.

Frameworks

♦ **Usability** - Frameworks that score highly here are ones that are easy to understand, use and deploy.

> # KEYPOINT:
>
> Key Framework comparison criteria:
>
> Strategic vs Project, Enterprise vs IT,
>
> Detail vs Usability.

Questions to Ponder

- ◆ Are these reasonable criteria?
- ◆ If not, what criteria would you use?
- ◆ How would you score each Framework?

			TOGAF	Zachman	PEAF
Transformation Focus		Strategic	2	8	10
		Project	5	8	2
Structural Focus		Enterprise	2	2	10
		IT	10	10	10
Conten		Detail	8	1	4
		Usability	1	1	10
		Total	28	30	46

© Pragmatic 365 (2008-2021)

Here we see the raw scores for each framework.

Of course you may have different views and can use the Framework Comparison Toolkit Spreadsheet in PEAF to modify them as you wish with a resulting changing of overall scores.

Frameworks

> # KEYPOINT:
>
> Raw Scores given by Pragmatic show
>
> PEAF in the lead.

Questions to Ponder

- ◆ Do you agree with the categories?
- ◆ If not, which would you remove or add?
- ◆ Why?
- ◆ Do you agree with these raw scores?
- ◆ If not how would you change them?
- ◆ Why did you change them in the way you did?

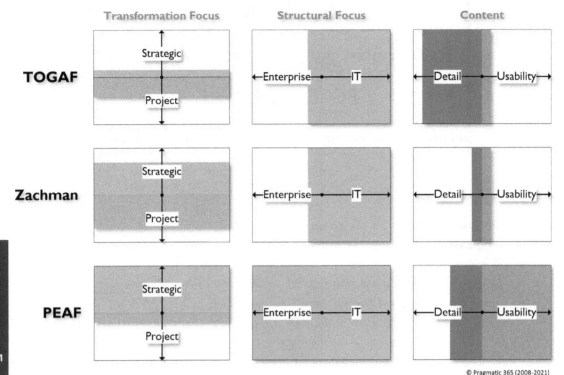

© Pragmatic 365 (2008-2021)

TOGAF

TOGAF's Transformational focus is mainly on the Solutioning and Elaboration phases of projects and the governance of Construction. It does cover Roadmapping to a small degree but only really from the point of Roadmapping for a very large project or a program. It doesn't cover Construction or Transitioning and its Structural focus is very IT oriented. It does provide a large amount of detail but largely because of this and other issues it is not very usable and difficult to implement.

Zachman

♦   Zachman's Transformational focus is largely strategic in nature and does cover most of the project domain but is very IT oriented. It doesn't provide much detail at all and not much guidance on how to use it either.

PEAF

♦   PEAF's Transformational focus is on the Strategising, Roadmapping and Governance of the Solutioning phases of the Transformation domain. Structurally it includes IT but is not limited to IT, instead covering the entire Enterprise domain. It offers a moderate amount of detail and concentrates mostly on the fundamentals that Enterprises need to get right. Because of this it is extremely usable and provides a lot of help to implement it - The Adoption section - which constitutes the Maturity Model.

KEYPOINT:

The EA framework you choose, depends on what you want from your EA framework.

ADOPTION:

EA Project Team: Decide what you want from an EA framework.

Questions to Ponder

♦ Do you agree with these overall ratings?
♦ If not, what would you change?

Frameworks

			Weighting	TOGAF	Zachman	PEAF
Transformation Focus		Strategic	5%	0.1	0.4	0.5
		Project	40%	2	3.2	0.8
Structural Focus		Enterprise	5%	0.1	0.1	0.5
		IT	5%	0.5	0.5	0.5
Conten		Detail	40%	3.2	0.4	1.6
		Usability	5%	0.05	0.05	0.5
		Total	100%	5.95	4.65	4.4

Even if you accept the raw scores provided by PEAF or change them, you may also place a different emphasis on each category, favouring some more than others. This will also change the resultant scores.

Here we see how the scores change if you make Project level guidance and Detail your preference.

> # KEYPOINT:
>
> If you favour Project guidance and Detail, rather than Strategic guidance and Usability – then TOGAF is clearly for you.

Questions to Ponder

- ◆ Are these weightings what you would choose?
- ◆ If not, what would you choose?

		Weighting	TOGAF	Zachman	PEAF
Transformation Focus	**Strategic**	30%	0.6	2.4	3
	Project	10%	0.5	0.8	0.2
Structural Focus	**Enterprise**	10%	0.2	0.2	1
	IT	10%	1	1	1
Conten	**Detail**	10%	0.8	0.1	0.4
	Usability	30%	0.3	0.3	3
	Total	100%	**3.4**	**4.8**	**8.6**

© Pragmatic 365 (2008-2021)

Here we see how the scores change if you make **Strategic** level guidance and **Usability** your preference.

Frameworks

> # KEYPOINT:
>
> If you favour Strategic guidance and Usability, rather than Project guidance and Detail – then PEAF is clearly for you.

Questions to Ponder

- ♦ What weightings would you assign to each category?
- ♦ Why?
- ♦ What is the result of those weightings?

Just done your *TOGAF®* training?
Great! Now what?

© Pragmatic 365 (2008-2021)

So, you've been on a TOGAF course. Great!

There are many good things in TOGAF, but being able to deploy and use them is a different ball game. Putting aside the conflicts of language within TOGAF created by the committees used to produce it, it does not explain how to adopt it very well. It is also missing some things of such fundamental importance, that using TOGAF without understanding these things and putting them in place will likely set you up for failure before you begin.

PEAF4TOGAF is a small subset of the PEFF/POET/PEAF content, specifically selected to help people who understand TOGAF, to deploy it and use it effectively.

> # KEYPOINT:
>
> PEAF provides the Bootstrap to kickstart your TOGAF adoption.

> # ADOPTION:
>
> Enterprise Architect: Use PEAF to set the context, to decide what parts of TOGAF to use where and when.

Questions to Ponder

- Have you used TOGAF?
- What did you do in the Preliminary Phase?
- Did you get the mandate and resources required to increase your maturity?

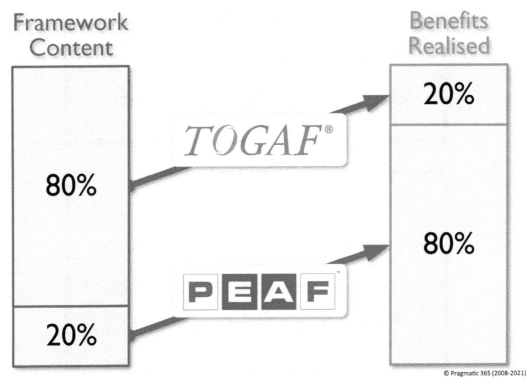

© Pragmatic 365 (2008-2021)

Here we illustrate a simple comparison between TOGAF and PEAF.

PEAF was never designed to be 100% complete or all encompassing. PEAF was built by an Enterprise Architect, for Enterprise Architects (or people wishing to move into that role, or management wishing to understand EA) in real world scenarios, by observing and experiencing EA failure, and then creating a **Pragmatic** set of fundamentals things to prevent other Enterprises making those same fundamental mistakes.

In comparison, TOGAF has been built by committee and aims to be 100% complete. In doing so, TOGAF has missed the 20% of the fundamentals things any Enterprise needs to get right, **BEFORE**, they start to expend 80% of the effort to gain the remaining 20% benefit.

In essence, if you have adopted PEAF, a case could be made to use TOGAF to gain the remaining 20% of benefit. However, as many Enterprises have found, adopting TOGAF before you have adopted PEAF is foolhardy - you cannot gain the remaining 20% of benefit before you have first put in the place the 20% (and gained the 80% benefit) of fundamentals that PEAF provides.

This is the reason why 99% of EA initiatives fail.

Not because they tried to adopt TOGAF.

But because they tried to adopt TOGAF, before adopting PEAF.

Another related point is that, because of TOGAF's size/complexity/detail, TOGAF requires a huge amount of customisation in order to adopt it. In addition, TOG provides nothing to aid an Enterprise in this regard. As a comparison, because of PEAF's simplicity, PEAF requires minimal customisation in order to adopt it. In addition, **Pragmatic** provides the **Pragmatic** Publishing Platform (**P3**) to allow Enterprises to not only customise it as they see fit, but to also publish the content to their intranet, produce physical and kindle books, and allows the creation and operation of in-house exams based on the customised content.

Many people say that no one is supposed to adopt TOGAF out-of-the-box, and in fact, adopting it out of the box is impossible.

PEAF can be adopted out-of-the-box.

KEYPOINT:

PEAF provides the 20% (fundamentals) that yields 80% of the benefit. TOGAF provides the 80% (details), that yields 20% of the benefit.

ADOPTION:

EA Project Team: Utilise PEAF to put in place the 20% (fundamentals) that yields 80% of the benefit.

Frameworks

Questions to Ponder

♦ Do you agree with this assertion?
♦ If not, why not, and how would you draw the diagram?

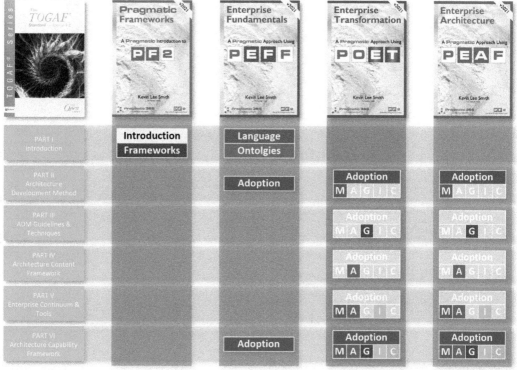

© Pragmatic 365 (2008-2021)

Here we see a high-level mapping of how TOGAF and the Pragmatic Frameworks relate to each other. It should be noted that POET and PEAF map to the same areas of TOGAF, but POET's content covers the whole of the Transformation capability (of which EA is only a part), whereas PEAF's content only covers the EA part.

- ♦ TOGAF Part I – Introduction, maps to the Introduction and Frameworks sections of PF2 and the Language and Ontologies sections of PEFF.
- ♦ TOGAF Part II – ADM, maps to the Adoption sections of PEFF, POET and PEAF (Preliminary phase), and the Methods sections of POET and PEAF.
- ♦ TOGAF Part III – ADM Guidelines & Techniques, maps to the Guidance sections of POET and PEAF.
- ♦ TOGAF Part IV – ACF, maps to the Artefacts sections of POET and PEAF.
- ♦ TOGAF Part V – Enterprise Continuum and Tools. It's difficult to map because it includes many different things. When it's talking about Tools, it maps to POET and PEAF's Items section. When it's talking about the information those tools manipulate, it maps to POET and PEAF's Artefacts section, and when it's talking about how to use those tools, it maps to POET and PEAF's Methods section.
- ♦ TOGAF Part VI – ACF, maps to the MAGIC of POET and PEAF (which define the Architecture Capability). It also maps to part of the Adoption parts of PEFF, POET and PEAF because it talks of maintain the Architecture capability.

As you can clearly see, the information for the Adoption of TOGAF is spread in multiple TOGAF sections whilst it is consistently identified in PEFF, POET and PEAF. This is perhaps one of the reasons what adopting TOGAF is so difficult.

Frameworks

KEYPOINT:

PEAF covers the whole of TOGAF

and more.

ADOPTION:

Enterprise Architect: Understand

which parts of PEAF to use to aid

TOGAF.

Questions to Ponder

- Have you used TOGAF?
- What did you do in the Preliminary Phase?
- Did you get the mandate and resources required to increase your maturity?

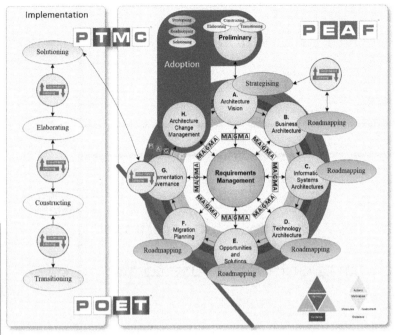

"PEAF is an EA bootstrap"

- Chris Forde
General Manager Asia Pacific & VP Enterprise Architecture The Open Group

© Pragmatic 365 (2008-2021)

Here we show how POET and PEAF compares to the TOGAF ADM.

Essentially, the Adoption Sections of POET and PEAF relate to the Preliminary phase of TOGAF. We also show how the Strategising and Roadmapping phases map to the meat of TOGAF, with the Governance and Lobbying disisplines of POET and PEAF map to Implementation Governance and Architecture Change Management.

Although I had thought of the phrase "an EA Bootstrap" before, Chris Forde independently thought of exactly the same phrase during discussions I had with him in April 2012.

POET also includes the other phases of Transformation (Engineering) that TOGAF lacks.

Pragmatic's frameworks are much more about making the necessary fundamental changes to an Enterprise's Transformation capability - defining what those changes are, why they are important and getting the mandate and resources to make those changes, so that the Enterprise can increase its Transformation Maturity to an appropriate level.

KEYPOINT:

Start with POET and PEAF, and then move on to TOGAF if required.

ADOPTION:

Enterprise Architect: If using TOGAF, use PEAF as a bootstrap

Questions to Ponder

- ◆ Have you used TOGAF?
- ◆ What did you do in the Preliminary Phase?
- ◆ Did you get the mandate and resources required to increase your maturity?

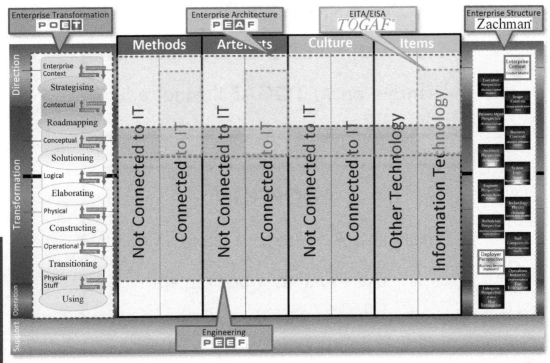

© Pragmatic 365 (2008-2021)

Here we show how other frameworks map on to the Transformation cascade (From strategy to Deployment) that POET defines.

The ellipses of POET show the phases of transformation while the rounded boxes show the models used. The boxes with square black lines are not models but actual physical things. In between each phase of transformation, we show the Governance and Lobbying disciplines of POET (using Transformation Debt™) which, as you will see later, is the key to making the whole coherent, connected and aligned.

The structure of the Enterprise is represented by the MAGIC of the Enterprise. Each of these is split into two categories. Things that are connected to (use) the IT of the Enterprise and things that are not. So, for example, there are Methods (Processes, etc) that are connected to (use) IT, but there are other processes in the Enterprise that are not connected to (use) IT. This is also true for The Artefacts and Culture columns. The Items column represents different technologies that the Enterprise uses and is split into one column for Information Technology, and one column for all other technologies (Mechanical, Electrical, Biological, Chemical, etc)

These categories will be used to overlap various frameworks on, so we can see where each fits and where the overlaps or gaps are.

The thick black line across the diagram marks the delineation between Project Portfolio Planning above and Project Execution below.

Zachman®

Zachman is an Enterprise Structure Framework, which maps almost one-to-one to POET's structural and transformational levels although we also show the missing Perspective and Model.

It should also be noted that this mapping is only general as there are other anomalies such as Zachman's Architect and Engineer perspectives (shown in Yellow and Green) which are actually fundamental perspectives which occur at all levels not just at one.

TOGAF®

TOGAF is mostly a Project IT Architecture (PITA) framework, for two reasons:

♦ **Vertically** although it includes some Roadmapping it is mainly concerned with projects, but only goes down to the Elaboration level, playing only a governance role to Construction and Transitioning.

♦ **Horizontally** the blue boxes show that it only covers IT things in the Items column and does not cover any other technologies. It only covers the Methods connected to IT, the Artefacts connected to IT and does not cover Culture at all.

PEAF™

PEAF is an Enterprise Architecture Framework, for two reasons:

♦ **Vertically** - it covers the Strategising and Roadmapping phases and is therefore concerned more with strategic cross-project things rather than tactical project-specific things. It is concerned with projects a little, but only from the EA Governance perspective - down to projects and Lobbying up from Projects - This is where the concept of Transformation Debt™ comes in that you will see later.

♦ **Horizontally** - it covers the entire enterprise including but NOT LIMITED to IT. It covers the MAGIC of the entire Enterprise.

PEEF™

PEEF is an Enterprise Engineering Framework, for two reasons:

♦ **Vertically** - it covers the Solutioning to Transitioning phases and is therefore concerned more with tactical project-specific things rather than strategic cross-project things. It is concerned with the entirety of projects.

♦ **Horizontally** - it covers the entire enterprise including but NOT LIMITED to IT.

Frameworks

> ## KEYPOINT:
>
> POET provides an Operating model for how Zachman, TOGAF, PEAF, COBIT, ITIL (and all other Transformation frameworks) relate to each other.

> ## ADOPTION:
>
> EA Project Team: Use POET as a canvas to understand how other frameworks you use, relate to each other.

Questions to Ponder

- Do you agree with this mapping? If not what would you change?
- Which Frameworks do you use?
- Which overall framework for Transformation do you use to map other to?

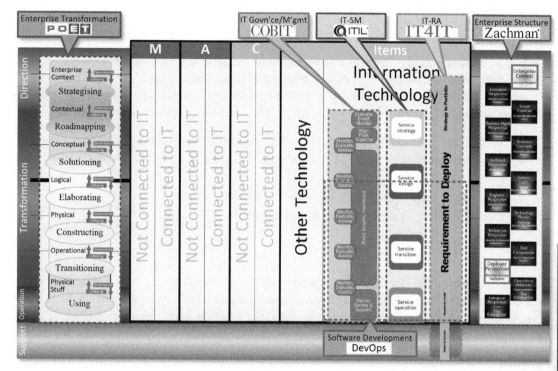

Here we show an expanded view of the IT part of the (technology) Items, to allow us to map COBIT® ITIL® and IT4IT®..

COBIT®

COBIT is an IT Governance & Management Framework, and covers Roadmapping and all project phases, plus the Operations domain (of IT Services). COBIT is an IT Governance & Management Framework, and covers four main domains:

- Evaluate Direct, Monitor (**EDM**) and Align, Plan Organise (**APO**) map to the Management domain of the Roadmapping level of POET.
- Build, Acquire, Implement (**BAI**) maps to the Management domain of the Roadmapping Solutioning, Elaborating, Constructing and Transitioning levels of POET.
- Monitor, Evaluate, Assess (**MEA**) maps to the Governance domain/interface between the Roadmapping Solutioning, Elaborating, Constructing Transitioning and Using levels of POET.
- Deliver Service & Support (**DSO**) maps to the Using domain of the Operation/Support domains of DOTS.

ITIL®

ITIL is a Service Management Framework. In its original form, it only covered the Service Operation or Management area, but over recent years has grown up the transformation stack although its domain is still only really IT Services.

- Service Strategy maps to the Roadmapping phase.
- Service Design maps to the Solutioning and Elaborating phases.
- Service Transition maps to the Constructing and Transitioning phases.

- ◆ Service Operations maps to the Operation domain.
- ◆

IT4IT®

IT4IT is a reference model for the IT used by the IT department of an Enterprise. Its width is narrow because it shows that it does not cover the IT for the entire Enterprise, but only the IT used for the IT department of the Enterprise. It does, however, extend up into the Roadmapping and Strategy phases, and down into the support area also.

- ◆ Strategy to Portfolio maps to the Strategising and Roadmapping phases.
- ◆ Requirement to Deploy maps to the Solutioning, Elaborating and Constructing phases.
- ◆ Request to Fulfil maps to the Operation domain.
- ◆ Detect to Correct maps to the Support domain.

DevOps

DevOps is a software development framework. It is a mindset, a culture, and a set of technical practices that combines software development (Dev) and information technology operations (Ops) to shorten the systems development life cycle while delivering features, fixes, and updates frequently .in close alignment with business objectives. Key aspects of DevOps are:

- ◆ Coding – Code development and review, source code management tools, code merging
- ◆ Building – Continuous integration tools, build status
- ◆ Testing – Continuous testing tools that provide feedback on business risks
- ◆ Packaging – Artefact repository, application pre-deployment staging
- ◆ Releasing – Change management, release approvals, release automation
- ◆ Configuring – Infrastructure configuration and management, infrastructure as code tools
- ◆ Monitoring – Applications performance monitoring, end-user experience

KEYPOINT:

Frameworks that span multiple domains (Transformation, Operation and Support) fragment the Enterprise.

ADOPTION:

Management: Consider using frameworks oriented around DOTS.

Questions to Ponder

- ◆ Do you agree with this mapping? If not what would you change?
- ◆ Which Frameworks do you use?
- ◆ Which overall framework for Transformation do you use to map other to?

Frameworks

Frameworks > Comparisons > TOGAF > Guidance vs Detail

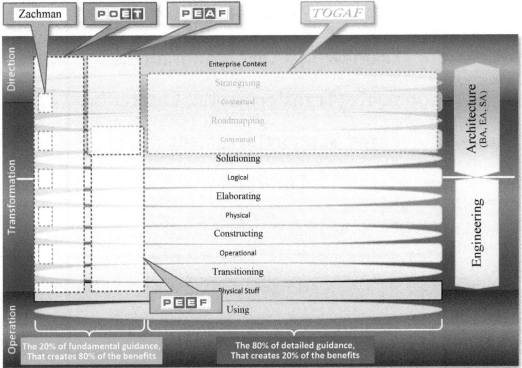

© Pragmatic 365 (2008-2021)

Here we compare frameworks in terms of the level of guidance they provide versus where they sit in the Transformation cascade (From Strategy to Deployment). The left of the diagram illustrates the 20% that provides 80% of the benefit. The right of the diagram illustrates the 80% that provides 20% of the benefit.

20% of

Zachman provides very low detail and only in the structural parts of the cascade. However, it is part of the 20% that provides 80% of the benefit.

POET provides more detail, and covers transformation as well as structure. It is part of the 20% that provides 80% of the benefit.

PEAF provides more detail again, but only in the domain of Enterprise Architecture - Strategy, Roadmapping and the Governance of those phases.

PEEF also provides more detail, but only in the domain of Enterprise Engineering - Solutioning, Elaborating, Constructing, Transitioning and the Governance of those phases.

Together they complete the 20% that provides 80% of the benefit.

TOGAF provides much more detail but only in Solutioning to Elaboration and the governance of Construction, although it does touch on Roadmapping. It effectively provides the remaining 80% that provides the remaining 20% of the benefit.

> ## KEYPOINT:
>
> POET/PEAF/PEEF provides the 20% (fundamentals) that yields 80% of the benefit. TOGAF provides the 80% (details), that yields 20% of the benefit.

> ## ADOPTION:
>
> Management: Decide what is more important – A) The 20% (fundamentals) that yields 80% of the benefit, or B) the 80% (details), that yields 20% of the benefit.

Questions to Ponder

- ♦ Where do the frameworks your Enterprise uses map onto this diagram?
- ♦ Do the frameworks you use cover the areas you need to cover?
- ♦ What do you use to guide the use of Frameworks?

Frameworks > Comparisons > TOGAF > Trends

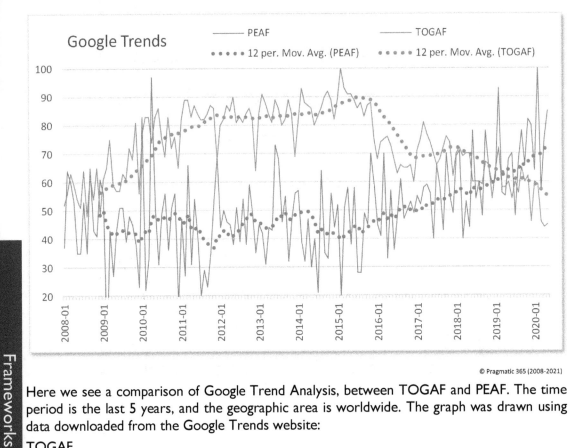

Here we see a comparison of Google Trend Analysis, between TOGAF and PEAF. The time period is the last 5 years, and the geographic area is worldwide. The graph was drawn using data downloaded from the Google Trends website:

TOGAF

> https://trends.google.com/trends/explore?date=2008-01-01%202020-05-27&q=togaf

PEAF

> https://trends.google.com/trends/explore?date=2008-01-01%202020-05-27&q=peaf

There can be many reasons why one trend is decreasing, while another is increasing, but we believe it is because after many years of TOGAF not delivering the value it promises, more and more people and Enterprises, are beginning to desire a more **Pragmatic** approach to Enterprise Architecture.

KEYPOINT:

The trend for TOGAF is falling. The Trend for PEAF is rising.

ADOPTION:

Management: Investigate why demand for TOGAF is falling, while demand for PEAF is rising.

Questions to Ponder

- ◆ Why do you think the trend for TOGAF is falling?
- ◆ Why do you think the trend for PEAF is rising?
- ◆ Do you agree with these trends?
- ◆ Have you experienced these trends?
- ◆ Do you think that investigating PEAF (and POET) to see how useful they are would be Pragmatic?

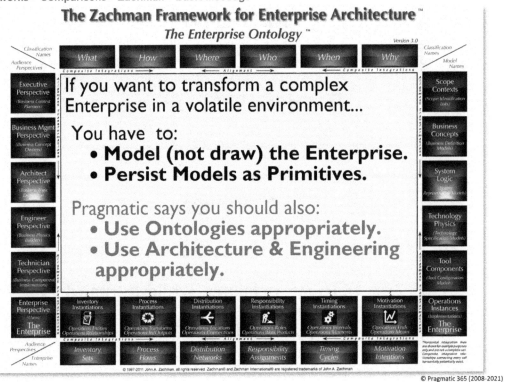

Although Enterprise Architecture is only a part of the entire Transformation domain, we mention Zachman here because whilst the Zachman Ontology is known as an Enterprise Architecture Ontology, and whilst John A. Zachman is deemed to be "The Father of Enterprise Architecture", it does in fact cover the whole Transformation domain (from Strategy to Deployment).

It is, in fact, an Enterprise Transformation Ontology where the top half covers Enterprise Architecture and the bottom half covers Enterprise Engineering (although the engineering part is IT focussed).

John A. Zachman is therefore "The Father of Enterprise Architecture" and "The Father of Enterprise Engineering"

The basic message contained in Zachman is that "You cannot change what you cannot see" and therefore is one of modelling and models - Architectural Models and Engineering Models.

POET and PEAF are built on the following conceptual ideas from the Zachman 6x6 grid:

1) Vertically - There are phases of Transformation that we need to consider - from the highest view of Enterprise Strategy to the physical deployment of change - and these phases must cover **ALL** the transformations we need to do to bridge that gap.

2) Horizontally - There are data used by each phase of transformation - that should be categorised - and these categorisations must cover **ALL** of the data we need for that phase.

Zachman teaches (quite correctly) that "If you want to transform a complex Enterprise in a volatile environment, you have to a) Model (not draw) the Enterprise, b) Persist Models as Primitives."

Modelling (not drawing) the enterprise means you need to make a distinction between drawings (which cannot be analysed or used in anyway) and models (which can be analysed and used in a multitude of ways) and therefore visual representations of things need a structured base.

Persisting models as primitives means that each element in a model should be stored as separate elements, which are then brought together to create one or more models.

If you are an IT person, you can think of the primitives as tables in a database and the models as SQL statements (or views) into those tables.

The other statements on this graphic relate to additional fundamental things that Zachman should explain but actually incorrectly explains the exact opposite.

Firstly, **Pragmatic** teaches us to "Use Ontologies appropriately". This means that an ontology should be used to create metamodels, which should be used to create models. Zachman incorrectly teaches people to create models based on the Zachman ontology (since he doesn't have a metamodel), instead of teaching people to create (and validate) metamodels on that ontology. This is because people want to create models and so since he only has an ontology, that is what is used.

Secondly, **Pragmatic** teaches us to "Use Architecture and Engineering appropriately". This means that Architecture and Engineering are closely related but totally different things. Confusing architecture and engineering and architects with engineers probably creates more problems in Enterprises than everything else put together. Can you imagine what would happen if you asked an Engineer to Architect a building or an Architect to Engineer it? When Zachman was asked in a classroom (not by me) to clarify what he meant by architecture and engineering (because he had been using those words a lot and it wasn't clear what he meant by them) Zachman replied "Oh well, some people say architecture, some people say engineering. They are the same thing really and I use the words interchangeably."

> # KEYPOINT:
>
> You can't change what you don't understand.
>
> You can't understand what you can't see.

> # ADOPTION:
>
> Management: Decide to move away from unstructured information, and towards modelling structured primitives.

Questions to Ponder

- ◆ Do you agree that "Modell (not draw) the Enterprise" and "Persist Models as Primitives" are the key messages that Zachman training delivers?
- ◆ If not, what other messages do you believe are important?

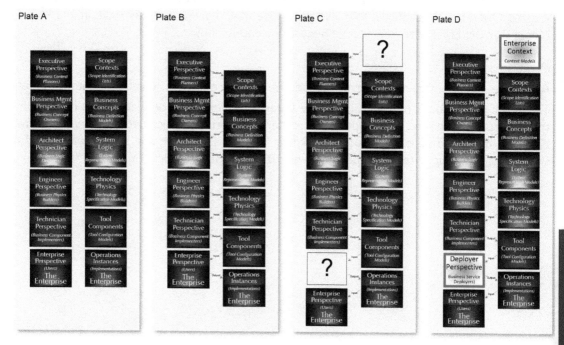

Plate A

Here we see the Zachman Ontology, showing the two labels used for each row. On the left is what is referred to as "Audience Perspectives" and on the right is what Z is referred to as "Model Names" or "Representations". These "Perspectives" and "Model Names" form a stack from high level strategy at the top to physical things in Operations at the bottom. The "Perspectives" on the left relate to people and therefore the work those people do. The "Model Names" on the right relate to the information those people use to do their work.

Because of this it is more apt to move the "Model Names" down a little to sit between each of the perspectives because each model forms the output from one perspective and the input to the next as illustrated in Plate B.

Plate B

As we move down these perspectives and models this makes sense:

♦ The Executives create the Context models...
♦ ...which are taken by Business Management as input who create Business Models...
♦ ...which are taken by Architects as input who create Logical Models...
♦ ...which are taken by Engineers as input who create Physical Models...
♦ ...which are taken by Technicians as input who create Configuration Models...
♦ ...which are taken by Users as input who create Operational Instances ?????????

Hang on ... that last one doesn't sound right at all ... users don't create Operational Instances ... Users use Operational instances ... so we need to move the User's Perspective down to the correct place.

Plate C

OK - that's better! Users take Operational Instances as their input and use them … correct!

But this creates a hole in our diagram - a Perspective that takes Configuration Models and creates Operational Instances. We also recognise that there is another hole at the top - a Model that the Enterprise Perspective needs to use as its input.

Plate D

And so we add the missing Deployer Perspective and the missing Enterprise Context Model.

To be fair to Zachman, he isn't missing the Enterprise Context Model per se, as he says that the enterprise's context is comprised of other Enterprises, which would have their own Zachman models. This is true, but as we know Context is King™, and so we really need to show it as, from our Enterprises perspective, it is the most important.

KEYPOINT:

In the Zachman

Framework/Ontology, the Deployer

perspective is missing.

ADOPTION:

Enterprise Architect: Be aware that

the Deployer perspective is missing.

Questions to Ponder

- Do you agree that the Deployer Perspective is missing in Zachman?
- If not, why not?
- If not, how to you reconcile the mismatches?

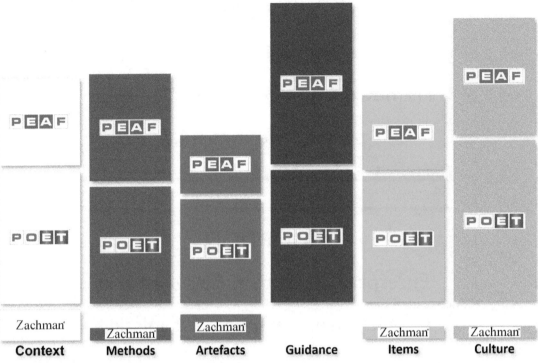

© Pragmatic 365 (2008-2021)

Here we see how the important seeds that John A. Zachman planted have been extended and built upon by POET and PEAF. Without Johns important work it is debatable whether POET and PEAF would even exist.

The height of each box is proportional to the quantity of material in each section.

The core of Zachman is an Enterprise Ontology which defines Artefacts hence the larger overlap with the Artefacts section of POET. However, it is only shown just over half width because Zachman is 5/6 Structural (What, How, Where, Who, When) and 1/6 Transformational (Why) which means it only covers just over half of the full Enterprise Transformation domain.

Whilst there is no methodological guidance in Zachman, there is a small overlap with the Methods section of POET because Zachman does define the notion of Transformational perspectives (Executive, Business Management, Architect, Engineer, Technician, Enterprise/Users). Context, Items and Culture are covered to a small degree in training although the Ontology itself does not.

KEYPOINT:

POET and PEAF greatly extends what Zachman provides.

ADOPTION:

Enterprise Architect: Use POET and PEAF to greatly extend what Zachman provides.

Questions to Ponder

- Do you agree that POET and PEAF greatly extends Zachman?
- If not, how would you map these things?
- What things do you think are in Zachman that do not exist in POET or PEAF?
- What things would you add to Zachman?

Frameworks > Comparisons > Zachman > Architect/Engineer

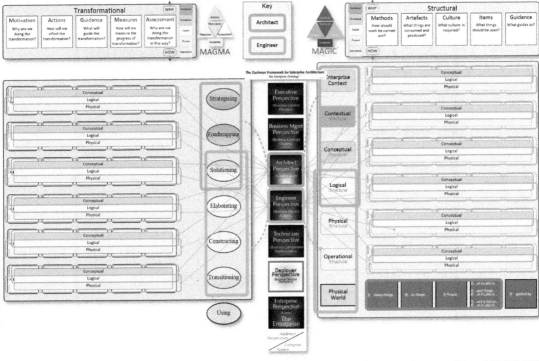

© Pragmatic 365 (2008-2021)

Here we see how the Zachman rows maps to the POET rows.

POET recognises two things about the Architect Perspective (row 3) in Zachman:

- ◆ An Architect's Perspective actually covers the **Strategising** to **Solutioning** Transformation phases, utilising the Structural information from the **Contextual** to **Logical** levels, driven by the **Enterprise Context**.
- ◆ An Architect's perspective also exists within all of these levels depending on whether the complexity of the work at each level warrants it.

POET recognises two things about the Engineer Perspective (row 4) in Zachman:

- ◆ An Engineer's Perspective actually covers the **Solutioning** to **Transitioning** Transformation phases, utilising the Structural information from the **Logical** to the **Physical World** levels, driven by the **Conceptual level**.
- ◆ An Engineer's perspective also exists within all of these levels depending on whether the complexity of the work at each level warrants it.

Having said that, there is another way too look at it...

If you consider Zachman's rows to be more like disciplines than a cascade of work (essentially take the word perspectives and apply it ruthlessly) then the Architect and Engineering rows are correct. If this is the case, then the order of the rows is irrelevant. Aka there is no meaning to one row being at the top and another row being further down.

There is an inference because the rows at the top are more likely to be done earlier and the rows at the bottom are more likely to be done later, but the Architect and Engineer rows (perspectives) could be applied at any time. In fact, the more I think about it, the more I think that the architect and engineer rows should not be rows but should be disciplines that could be utilised on any of the other perspectives.

This would mean that we need new names for the architect and Engineer perspectives. Designer and Builder sound like good ones to me. So, we end up with something like the graphic below.

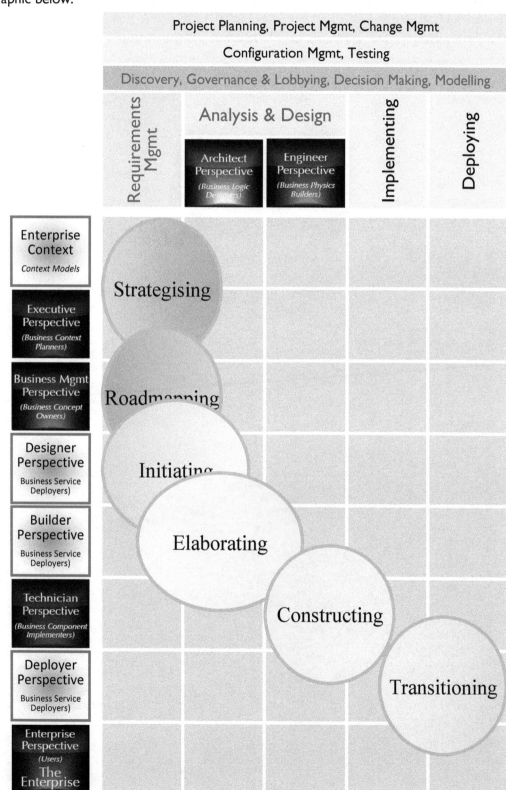

So, what this diagram illustrates, is that we consider the Architects and Engineers "perspectives" more as disciplines rather than phases, while we consider the other perspectives, more as perspectives rather than disciplines, but those perspectives map one2one with Phases.

I feel we are getting further, but I also feel I have not found the most elegant description.

KEYPOINT:

Zachman's Architect and Engineer rows are wrong, because Architecture and Engineering can be performed at any row.

ADOPTION:

Enterprise Architect: Be aware that Zachman's Architect and Engineer rows are wrong, because Architecture and Engineering can be performed at any row.

Frameworks

Questions to Ponder

- ◆ Do you agree that Zachman's Architect and Engineer rows are wrong?
- ◆ If not, how would you map these things?

Frameworks > Comparisons > Zachman > Why/How

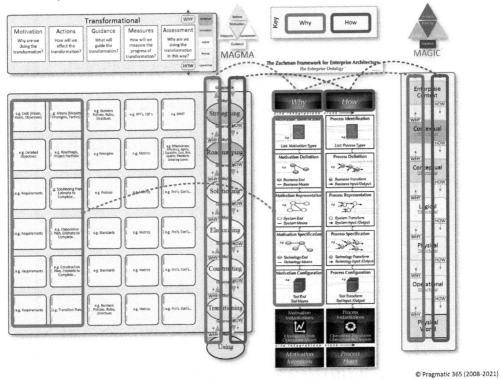

© Pragmatic 365 (2008-2021)

Firstly, at a general level, POET recognises that **Why** and **How** actually exist from level to level rather than just as a column. For each level, **How** that level is achieved is defined by the level below it and **Why** that level is the way it is, is defined by the level above it.

Secondly, in general terms, it would seem sensible that the **Why** column should map to the **Motivation** column of MAGMA - however, examining the descriptions in each of the cells under the **Why** column reveals a mixture of **Means** and **Ends**, hence the **Why** column actually maps to the **Motivation** and **Actions** columns of MAGMA.

Finally, rows 1 and 2 of the **Why** column speak specifically of **Business Means** and **Business Ends**, hence they actually map to the **Motivation** (ends) and **Actions** (means) of only the **Strategising** level of POET.

> # KEYPOINT:
>
> Zachman's Why and How columns, only equate to the Motivation and Actions of MAGMA.
>
> Why and How are also questions answered by moving up and down the rows, not columns.

> # ADOPTION:
>
> Enterprise Architect: Be aware that Zachman's Why column contains Means (How) and Ends (Why), and the How column relates to the Methods of the thing in question, not the How of Transformation.

Questions to Ponder

- ♦ Do you agree that Zachman's Why and How columns are a little strange?
- ♦ If not, how would you map these things?

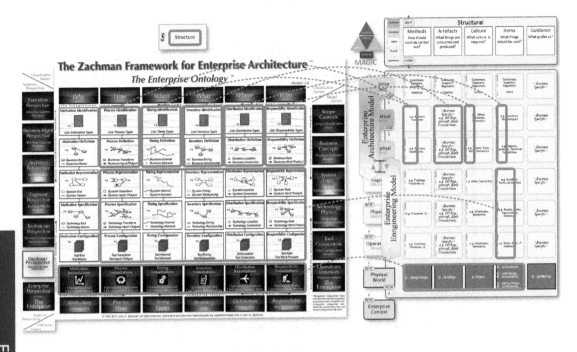

Here we map the Zachman Ontology to the structural Ontology of POET:

- ◆ Rows 1 and 2 map to the top two levels of MAGIC (**Contextual** and **Conceptual**) but not completely:
  - ◆ The **How** and **When** columns talk of processes and therefore map only to the Process sub-domain of the **Methods** domain of MAGIC.
  - ◆ The **What** column talks in terms of business entities and therefore maps to the **Artefact** domain of MAGIC.
  - ◆ The **Where** column talks in terms of location and therefore maps only to the Location sub-domain of the **Items** domain of MAGIC.
  - ◆ The **Who** talks in terms of people and therefore maps only to the people sub-domain of the **Culture** domain of MAGIC.
- ◆ Rows 3, 4 and 5 map directly to the **Logical**, **Physical** and **Operation** levels in MAGIC, however only in relation to IT as those rows only talk in terms of systems and technologies.
- ◆ Row 6 maps directly to the **Physical World** level of MAGIC.

KEYPOINT:

Zachman's top two rows equate to MAGIC but the lower down you go the more IT specific it becomes.

ADOPTION:

Enterprise Architect: Be aware that Zachman's rows, get more IT specific the further down you go.

Questions to Ponder

♦ Do you agree that Zachman gets more IT centric the further down you go?
♦ If not, why not? How would you map these things?

Frameworks > Comparisons > Zachman > Perspectives and Models

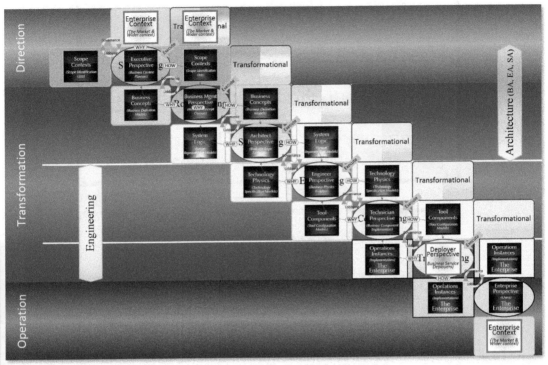

Here we see the holistic and coherent cascade of phases and models that POET defines, from Strategic intent at the top, down to deployed change at the bottom, and how the Zachman Models and Perspectives relate to them.

Zachman only references the perspectives, and not the transformations that need to occur at each level. In addition, Zachman also only references current state information related to each perspective and not the target (or intermediate) Structural states.

> # KEYPOINT:
>
> Zachman's (corrected) perspectives and models can be mapped to the Phases and Levels of POET.

> # ADOPTION:
>
> Enterprise Architect: Be aware that Zachman's (corrected) perspectives map one to one with POETS Phases

Frameworks

Questions to Ponder

♦ Do you agree that Zachman's (corrected) perspectives map one to one with POET phases?

♦ If not, how would you map these things?

Frameworks > Adoption > Overview

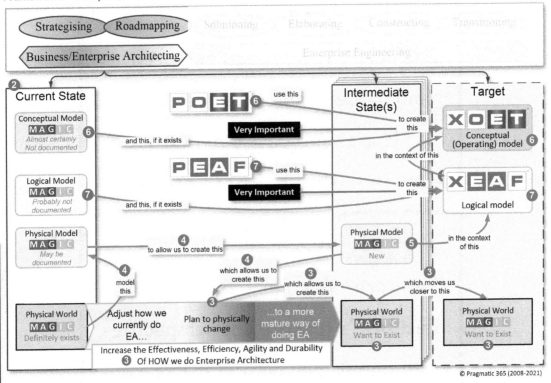

© Pragmatic 365 (2008-2021)

Let's walk through what happens when we want to improve any domain in the Enterprise.

♦ 1 - Here we see some phases of work going on in Domain 1 and Domain 2. These Domains represents some part of the Enterprise we are looking to improve, e.g. Credit Card Processing, Renting Cars, Delivering Packages, Drilling for Oil, Selling Books, etc.
Let's focus on Domain 1, and consider HOW that work is physically done, and how models that describe HOW that work is being done can be represented at different levels of abstraction.

- 2 - The actual work being done in the Physical world is represented by the box at the bottom in grey. This work can be represented in models at different levels of abstraction (Idealisation/Realisation): Physical model (green), Logical model (yellow), and Conceptual model (orange). In each model we describe information about:
  - The Methods being used in Domain 1.
  - The Artefacts being produced and consumed by Domain 1.
  - The Guidance (Principles, Policies, Standard) used guide Domain 1.
  - The Items (Technology) used execute the Methods of Domain 1.
  - The Culture (People) used execute the Methods of Domain 1.

So let's now consider, for a typical Enterprise, which of these models (that describe how Domain 1 is performed) exist.
  - The Physical model (green) for Domain 1 almost certainly exists.
  - The Logical model (yellow) for Domain 1 also probably exists.
  - The Conceptual model (orange) for Domain 1 may exist.

- 3 - If we identify a need to increase the Effectiveness, Efficiency, Agility and Durability of **HOW** Domain 1 is done, this means we need to adjust **HOW** we currently do Domain 1. From **HOW** we currently do it, to a more mature way of doing it. This increase in maturity is likely to not be a one-shot deal, but instead we will have a long-term target, with one or more intermediate states that we wish to progress through over time. To effect change, we need a plan to describe exactly how we will effect that change.

- 4 - In order to create that plan to physically change, it would be lunacy to just wade in and start changing things in the Physical World, so first we need to determine the new Physical model of what that Intermediate State needs to be, and this new Physical model needs to be created in the context of what currently exists, the old Physical model.

- 5 – In order for us to be able to create a new physical model we need some higher level guidance. Therefore, this new Physical model needs to be created in the context of a longer term VERY IMPORTANT Logical model, which in turn needs to exist in the context of a longer term and wider scope VERY IMPORTANT Conceptual model. But why are these Logical and Conceptual models needed and why are they so important?
  - Because they define the bigger picture both in terms of time and scope.
  - Without a Target Logical model, any changes will tend to ignore future changes, meaning any changes may be good for today, but compromise tomorrow.
  - Without a Target Conceptual model, any changes will tend to ignore how Domain 1 fits into the wider domain including Domain 2. If this is not done, we could be improving **HOW** Domain 1 is done, but negatively impacting Domain 2, thereby optimizing the part but de-optimising the whole.

- 6 - So how should the **VERY IMPORTANT** Conceptual model be created? If you already have a Conceptual model (Operating model) for Domain 1, and it is of appropriate maturity, then you have no need to create one or modify it. You can just use it.
  However, if you do not have one of appropriate maturity, then you need to create one. This is done by taking an Industry Framework (**best practice**) and tailoring it to

be your Modified Industry Framework. And that is done in the context of taking into account the Current Conceptual model for Domain 1.

♦ 7 - So how should the **VERY IMPORTANT** Logical model be created?
If you already have a Logical model for Domain 1, and it is of appropriate maturity, then you have no need to create one or modify it. You can just use it.
However, if you do not have one of appropriate maturity, then you need to create one. This is done by taking an Industry Framework (best practice) and tailoring it to be your Modified Logical Framework. And that is done in the context of taking into account the Current Logical model for Domain 1.

The approach we have thus far defined, applies to us changing (maturing) any part (domain) of the Enterprise. Therefore, the approach we follow when changing (maturing) the Transformation or Enterprise Architecture part (domain) of the Enterprise is exactly the same. i.e. We should be eating-our-own-dogfood.

♦ 1 - Here we see the phases of work going on in the Enterprise Architecting and Enterprise Engineering Domains.
Let's focus on the BA/EA domain, and consider HOW that work is physically done, and how models that describe HOW that work is being done can be represented at different levels of abstraction.

♦ 2 - The actual work being done in the Physical world is represented by the box at the bottom in grey. This work can be represented in models at different levels of abstraction (Idealisation/Realisation): Physical model (green), Logical model (yellow), and Conceptual model (orange).

  ♦ The Physical model (green) for BA/EA may exist in some form, possibly in terms of RACI matrices or process diagrams, but for most Enterprises this information is in the heads of the people performing the tasks and is not explicitly modelled.

  ♦ The Logical model (yellow) for BA/EA may also exist but more often does not.

  ♦ The Conceptual model (orange) for BA/EA will almost certainly not exist and in most Enterprises has not even been considered.

NOTE: It is important to note how the existence of the information that describes the **BA/EA** domain, contrasts with the existence of the information that describes most other domains. For most other domains, they tend to be modelled reasonably well, but for the **BA/EA** domain (and the wider Transformation Domain) the models tend to be a lot sparser, if they exist at all. This is evidence of the immaturity of the **BA/EA** capability in most Enterprises. Evidence of us **NOT** eating-out-own-dogfood.

♦ 3 - If we identify a need to increase the Effectiveness, Efficiency, Agility and Durability of **HOW** BA/EA is done, this means we need to adjust **HOW** we currently do BA/EA. From **HOW** we currently do it, to a more mature way of doing it. This increase in maturity is likely to not be a one-shot deal, but instead we will have a long-term target, with one or more intermediate states that we wish to progress through over time. To effect change, we need a plan to describe exactly how we will effect that change.

♦ 4 - In order to create that plan to physically change, it would be lunacy to just wade in and start changing things in the Physical World, so first we need to determine the new Physical model of what that Intermediate State needs to be, and this new

Physical model needs to be created in the context of what currently exists, the old Physical model.

5 – In order for us to be able to create a new physical model we need some higher-level guidance. Therefore, this new Physical model needs to be created in the context of a longer-term **VERY IMPORTANT** Logical model, which in turn needs to exist in the context of a longer term and wider scope **VERY IMPORTANT** Conceptual model. But why are these Logical and Conceptual models needed and why are they so important?

- Because they define the bigger picture both in terms of time and scope.
- Without a Target Logical model, any changes will tend to ignore future changes, meaning any changes may be good for today, but compromise tomorrow.
- Without a Target Conceptual model, any changes will tend to ignore how BA/EA fits into the wider domain including Enterprise Engineering. If this is not done, we could be improving **HOW** BA/EA is done, but negatively impacting Enterprise Engineering, thereby optimizing the part but de-optimising the whole.

- 6 - So how should the **VERY IMPORTANT** Conceptual model be created?
  If you already have a Conceptual model (Operating model) for BA/EA, and it is of appropriate maturity, then you have no need to create one or modify it. You can just use it.

  However, if you do not have one of appropriate maturity, then you need to create one. This is done by taking an Industry Framework (**POET**) and tailoring it to be your Modified Industry Framework. And that is done in the context of taking into account the Current Conceptual model for BA/EA.

- 7 - So how should the **VERY IMPORTANT** Logical model be created?
  If you already have a Logical model for BA/EA, and it is of appropriate maturity, then you have no need to create one or modify it. You can just use it.

  However, if you do not have one of appropriate maturity, then you need to create one. This is done by taking an Industry Framework (**PEAF**) and tailoring it to be your Modified Logical Framework. And that is done in the context of taking into account the Current Logical model for BA/EA.

Frameworks

Frameworks

> # KEYPOINT:
>
> Use POET as a conceptual guide.

> # ADOPTION:
>
> EA Project Team: Use POET as the
> Conceptual target, to figure out the
> physical changes required to your
> Transformation capability's Methods,
> Artefacts, Culture and Environment.

Questions to Ponder

♦ Does this approach look familiar?
♦ What approach does your Enterprise take when maturing parts of it?
♦ How well is your EA capability (and the wider Transformation capability) modelled in your Enterprise?
♦ Is your Enterprise's Transformation capability, eating-its-own-dogfood?
♦ If not, what problems does that create? What needs to be done to fix it

Frameworks > Adoption > Mapping

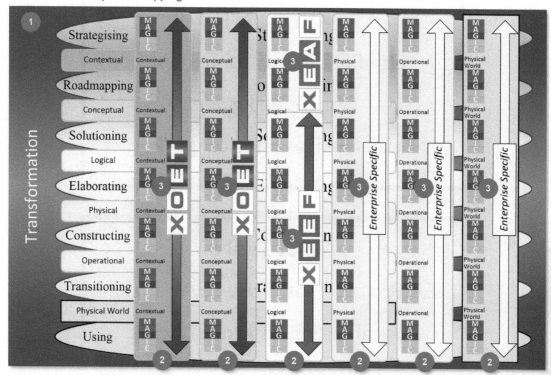

© Pragmatic 365 (2008-2021)

Here we see the output of utilising POET and PEAF, and how the creation and utilisation of XOET (an Enterprises Operating model for Enterprise Transformation, based on POET) and XEAF (which is an Enterprises Enterprise Architecture Framework, based on PEAF) plays out.

1 - The diagram represents the Transformation capability of an Enterprise, comprising 6 phases (Strategising, Roadmapping, Solutioning, Elaborating, Constructing and Transitioning) and takes information though 5 levels of abstraction (Contextual, Conceptual, Logical, Physical, Operational) culminating in physical changes at the bottom.

2 - We can model these phases of Transformation at different levels of abstraction (Contextual, Conceptual, Logical, Physical, Operational), and for each level of abstraction, we can model the MAGIC for each phase.

3 - We can now show:

- ◆ a) How XOET provides the models at the Contextual and Conceptual levels for all phases of the transformation domain
- ◆ b) How XEAF provides the logical model for the Strategising and Roadmapping phases (EA) and,
- ◆ c) How XEEF provides the logical model for the project phases of Solutioning, Elaborating, Constructing and Transitioning.

We can also see that The Physical model, Operational model and Physical World levels are Enterprise specific, because this level of detail is generally different for each Enterprise, but is created by the Enterprise, under the guidance of the models above them provided by XOET, XEAF and XEEF.

KEYPOINT:

Use POET as a Contextual /
Conceptual guide.

Use PEAF as a logical guide.

ADOPTION:

EA Project Team: Use PEAF as the
Logical target, to figure out the
physical changes required to your EA
capability's Methods, Artefacts,
Culture and Environment.

Questions to Ponder

- Does this approach look familiar?
- What approach does your Enterprise take when maturing parts of it?

APPENDIX

KEYPOINT:

The Appendix section contains

information on the background of

PF2, POET, PEAF and the author.

WHY?	• We Care About Enterprises • We Care About the People who Direct, Operate, Transform and Support Enterprises

WHEN?	• PEAF 2008	• POET 2014	• PTMC 2018

WHERE?	• Born from Observing Failure

HOW?	• 150,000 Hours of Thinking • 20,000 Hours of Creating

USING WHAT?	• Architecture, Engineering, Altruism • Honesty, Integrity, Persistence, Passion • Common Sense, Logic

© Pragmatic 365 (2008-2021)

Why Were They Created?

Because I care. Because I care about Enterprises. Because I care about the people who **Direct, Operate, Transform** and **Support** Enterprises. Because I am angry about how much time is wasted. Because I am angry about how much money is wasted. From the Afghani to the Zloty, I guarantee you are wasting it. Big time!

This work was inspired by all those who seek to make the world a better place rather than those that seek to own it.

When Were They Created?

PEAF was initially launched in November 2008 and POET in 2014.

Where Did They Come From?

All **Pragmatic** Ontologies and Frameworks were created from observing failure. That is:

- ◆ Seeing why people fail
- ◆ What problems they encounter
- ◆ Providing things to reduce the risk of others failing in the same way
- ◆ Providing things to alleviate the problems people have.

Around 2002 I began to be interested in something called "Enterprise Architecture". The term started to appear more in publications and people started to talk about it more - although from listening to them there never seemed to be a concrete definition of what it actually was that everyone agreed with (some say that's still the case today!). Using logic and common sense I could surmise that it was not Project level Architecture (because that already had a name - Solution Architecture) and therefore it must be something at a "higher level" - not just bigger. Something related to:

♦ What goes on before projects execute and before Solution Architects start working on those projects.

♦ Enterprise Centric, or more specifically Enterprise Transformation Centric, rather than Project Centric and/or IT Centric.

At that time it all seemed to be a bit of a black art (some say it still is!) and so, being an Architect and not wanting to reinvent the wheel (others call it being lazy!), I surmised that there must be something out there (a bit like Prince or ITIL or MSP for example) - a framework - that might help people to "do" EA by:

♦ Helping people understand what EA was.

♦ Helping people increase the maturity in how an Enterprise "does" EA.

So, I consulted the mighty Google (sorry Oracle!). Google told me about something called Zachman and something called TOGAF. And so I went off to investigate further.

From what I could tell, Zachman's message seemed to resonate well with me in terms of general thinking I had built up over the preceding 20 years, namely:

♦ You can't change what you can't see - hence the need to model things - in a structured way.

♦ There must be Phases involved in Transformation to get from Strategic intent at the top down to real physically deployed things at the bottom.

These basic messages haven't changed and are as valid today as they always were - although the important distinction between Enterprise Architecture and Enterprise Engineering that **Pragmatic** makes today was not (and still is not) recognised in Zachman (despite my attempts to do so). But, whilst these fundamental things (modelling and phases/levels) were a good start, they were much too high level to provide any practical help in using them (which is what a framework is supposed to do) and so I invested more time looking into the much more detailed TOGAF.

As I looked into TOGAF, the first thing that struck me was "Where the hell do I start?". The material was immense, complex, confusing, very dry, hard to consume and offered no guidance about how to adopt it. So, assuming it was my ignorance that was the problem I booked myself on a TOGAF course. Within the first 2 hours of the first day it became clear that it was centred around Project level IT centric Architecture.

Nothing wrong with Project level IT centric Architecture, but not Enterprise Architecture.

Fantastic for those Enterprises that had still not figured out that the complexity of the IT landscape had grown to such a level that using Architecture as a discipline on IT Projects (Solution Architecture) was almost mandatory (unless you wanted to waste a shed load of money and deliver a shed load of bad IT to customers), but not Enterprise Architecture.

Great for those Enterprise that wanted to formalise their Solution Architecture discipline, but not Enterprise Architecture.

Great for those Enterprises that wanted to continue to treat "The Business" as a second class citizen to "IT", but not Enterprise Architecture.

At least not the Enterprise Architecture that logic and common sense dictated to me.

Anyway, I got through the course, passed the exams and became TOGAF Certified. Over the next few years I worked at various organisations and my TOGAF certification served me well in terms of getting me job interviews and most of the subsequent contracts. Having got a contract (because I was TOGAF certified) I then endeavoured to first discover how much and what parts of TOGAF were being used. The conversation (over many days, sometimes weeks) usually went something like this:

K: "Hi Allen, I'm new here. I've been told that you use TOGAF, can you tell me what parts you are using and which you aren't?"

A: "Hi Kevin, Errrmm, Yeah sure - you need to talk to Steve, he's the one that did the training."

<time passes....>

K: "Hi Steve, I'm new here. I've been told that you use TOGAF, can you tell me what parts you are using and which you aren't?"

S: "Hi Kevin, Errrmm, why are you asking me?"

K: "Allen told me you did the training and you would know."

S: "Err yeah, but I was only one of the twenty people who did it, I wasn't the main person. Listen - I'm a bit busy on this CRM project at the moment, can you go and ask James about it - I think he was the main guy."

<time passes....>

K: "Hi James, I'm new here. I've been told that you use TOGAF, can you tell me what parts you are using and which you aren't?"

J: "Hi Kevin, Errrmm, why are you asking me?"

K: "Steve told me you did the training and you were the main guy so you would know."

J: "Err yeah, but I was moved off that onto this ESB project. Listen - I'm a bit busy at the moment, Dave took over that TOGAF thing - go talk to Dave."

<time passes....>

K: "Hi Dave, I'm new here. I've been told that you use TOGAF, can you tell me what parts you are using and which you aren't?"

D: "Hi Kevin, Errrmm - why are you asking me?"

K: "James told me you did the training and you're now the guy in charge of TOGAF adoption."

D: "Err No! That's Chris, you need to talk to Chris"

<time passes....>

K: "Hi Chris, I'm new here. I've been told that you use TOGAF, can you tell me what parts you are using and which you aren't?"

C: "Hi Kevin, Errrmm, why are you asking me?"

K: "James told me Dave did the training and he was the guy in charge of TOGAF adoption, but that Dave says it wasn't him, it was you"

C: "Err Yeah - well I went on the course, but to be honest we never did anything about if after that, you should go talk to Allen, he knows what's going on"

In every case, after being passed from pillar to post, it always transpired that no one was actually using TOGAF at all.

So, I began to build up my own intellectual capital (documents, checklists, presentations, spreadsheets, ideas, concepts, processes, products, etc) so that I could bring them to bear as a set of quick start artefacts for subsequent contracts.

During 2008 it suddenly dawned on me that all this intellectual capital that I had built up, actually constituted what I thought an EA framework should contain. So, in addition to cleaning up and structuring the material so others could adopt and use it easily, I had to choose a name. So, I thought, what one word would sum up my approach? A core of fundamental things - the 20% that would give 80% of the benefit - that would reduce or remove 20% of the risks that cause 80% of the failures. Cutting through all the smoke and mirrors and Cutting EA to the Bone. And so the name **Pragmatic** chose me.

How Were They Created?

POET and PEAF have taken more than 10,000 hours to produce in terms of physical work, born from approximately 150,000 hours of thinking. The graphics were not just drawn - like most good things they evolved - and while many of them look quite simple, it took an awful lot of work and pain to get to those simple graphics. To an outside observer, those diagrams could appear as if someone just sat down and drew them but each one has had many versions as it has evolved, coalesced, fragmented, reconstituted, gone down the wrong track, fragmented, coalesced again and then finally thrown away, only to be resurrected when a light bulb went on somewhere in the deepest darkest recesses of my feeble brain.

Elegance and simplicity takes a lot of hard work to achieve but, anything **Pragmatic** must be so.

"Je n'ai fait celle-ci plus longue que parce que je n'ai pas eu le loisir de la faire plus courte."

- Blaise Pascal ("Lettres Provinciales", 1657)

Which loosely translates to

"If I Had More Time, I Would Have Written a Shorter Letter"

In fact, the amount of things and work I have thrown away greatly outweighs what now exists.

I believe that POET and PEAF have achieved elegance and simplicity to some degree but, of course, "we don't live in a perfect world" (as so many Managers I have worked for in the past have reminded me on so many occasions) and there is always more work to do. POET and PEAF will evolve, as everything must do, but for now, it is good enough.

With the benefit of time to think of a suitable response to those Managers, my response now would be:

"We don't live in a perfect world?
I know - Believe me I know!
If we did, we wouldn't be having this conversation ;-)"

What Was Used to Create Them?

Basically, common sense. It has always amazed me, how many things in business (and in life) do not seem to adhere to any common sense at all, which probably explains why a lot of things that are created to help people improve or mature something, contain a lot of common sense. In addition I have a brain split into two parts (Architecture and Engineering) that work together but also conflict a lot of the time. But it is from this conflict that progress lies.

Methods

♦ Architecture, Engineering, Logic.

Artefacts

♦ Input - Air, Water, Nespresso, Earl Grey, Toast, Ham Eggs & Chips, Bombay Sapphire (Tonic), Johnny Walker Black Label (Coke Zero), Whiskers, Paper, Ink, Blood, Sweat, Tears.

♦ Output - PF2 Book, POET Book, PEAF Book, **Pragmatic365**.org Website

Guidance

♦ Common Sense, W.E. Deming, J. Zachman, T. Graves.

Items

♦ Biological Technology - Kevin - Generally all of him, but mostly his brain, eyes and hands. (His stomach, colon and bladder put in an appearance occasionally, with his posterior providing a supporting role :-), Murphy the cat.

♦ Mechanical Technology - 25 Buttermere, Braintree, Essex, CM77 7UY, UK, Desk, Chair, Whiteboard (Pens and Eraser).

♦ Electrical - Challenge Fan Heater, Creative GigaWorks T40 Series II 2.0 PC Speakers

♦ Information Technology
  ♦ Hardware - Dell Latitude E6520 (Intel i7-2760QM @ 2.4GHz, 8GB RAM), 2 * 32in 2560x1600 LED Monitors, 2 * 24in 1920x1200 LED Monitors, HP Officejet Pro X576, Samsung Galaxy Note 8.
  ♦ Software - MS Windows 10, MS Visio, MS Word, MS Excel, MS PowerPoint, Paint.NET, Integromat, CognitoForms
  ♦ Languages – VBA, VBscript, Javascript, SQL, ASP, HTML, CSS
  ♦ Data – (mp3) David Bowie, Pet Shop Boys, Dean Martin, Chris Rea.

Culture

♦ God, Honesty, Integrity, Pragmatism, Altruism, Persistence, Passion, Psychology

> # KEYPOINT:
>
> Use POET and PEAF to make sure
>
> you don't make the mistakes that
>
> cause 90% of all EA initiatives to fail.

Questions to Ponder

- ◆ Do you think that observing failure is a good way to figure out how to improve things?
- ◆ What failures have you witnessed in the past?
- ◆ What does that tell you about how to improve it?

- # Kevin Lee Smith

- # 40 Years in all phases of Enterprise Transformation

- # MBTI: (INTJ) Mastermind, (INTP) Architect

- # DISC: (7414) Result-Oriented

- # Belbin: Plant, Shaper

© Pragmatic 365 (2008-2021)

Who Created The Pragmatic Family of Frameworks (PF2)?

A simple man.

My career began at the age of 16 in 1978 as an Electrical and Electronic Apprentice with Marconi Radar Systems (Blackbird Road, Leicester, UK) At that time I was really into electronics and had been playing with little circuits for a few years. It was really exciting. I spent my time between college and "The Factory" where I got the chance to work in many different departments. It was really exciting. Around 1980 I ended up in a Department (New Parks, Leicester UK) called TEPIGEN (**TE**levision **PI**cture **GEN**erator) who had built the visual system for a ship simulator. Six million Pounds of custom built hardware (that had less processing power than the CPU in the phone that's in your pocket) consisting mainly of four racks of "Picture Processors" (Motorola 68000s) driven by a PDP11. It was really exciting. The output was on three channels each delivering 40 degrees field of view which drove three large Barco projectors. Interestingly at one point there were black speckles that kept appearing on the displays, moving about in random patterns and appearing and disappearing in the same apparently random fashion. After months of software and hardware investigation the problem was identified. It was a test Radar across the apron from where our Portacabins where located that was spraying us periodically with microwaves! It was really exciting.

I began my time there hand entering the data which described the terrain and buildings and which fed the picture processors, and wrote my first program in DEC BASIC. Over the next four years or so my programming skills grew, and I moved from BASIC to FORTRAN and then to PASCAL. It was really exciting. The ship simulator turned into a flight simulator which meant it was the biggest video game in the world. It was really exciting. So much so that I would work late into the night (sometimes 48 hours at a stretch) and go into work on Saturdays or Sundays. Right from the beginning it wasn't so much the code I wrote that I got excited about it was more HOW I wrote the code that interested me. I would often spend hours writing a program and finally get it working, only to tear it to pieces and rewrite it in a new and elegant way, often with more features, less code and more opportunity to reuse things later. It was really exciting. Even at that time I spent more time throwing things away than I spent creating things. I believe this is where progress comes from. Sounds totally counter-intuitive I know, but most things of value are counter-intuitive!

Around 1986 the plug was pulled on TEPIGEN and I moved to another department (Fleet, Hampshire, UK) who produced a system called TELEVIEW (an improvement on Teletext and a forerunner of "The Web") for Singapore's Telecom Company (SingTel). I had moved on to C as a programming language. The most elegant and powerful language I have ever used. It took me a while to understand it but after reading the perfect "The C Programming Language" (Kernighan and Ritchie) the penny dropped. It was really exciting.

A brief spell at SD Scicon (1989-1991) was followed by three years working for Deutsche Bank (Singapore) where I found the best food in the world and where my architectural tendencies came to the fore. It was really exciting. While there I created and sold a numerical analysis package for lottery numbers called Mega4D. Returning in 1994 I spent six years working for Eurobase Systems (Chelmsford, UK) doing Application Architecture and creating Architectural and programming frameworks.

From 2000 to 2011 I spent my time working for various Enterprises as a contractor. While interesting, it wasn't very exciting, but all the time, whatever domain I worked in I was always interested in improving it. Each time this met a limit and the limit was always as a consequence of things being done less than effectively and less than efficiently in the preceding step. Hence my roles moved from Application Architecture, Data Architecture and Technology Architecture into Technical Architecture (a bit of a misnomer!) then Solution Architecture then Enterprise Architecture and finally the entire Transformation domain.

Since 2011 I have devoted my time to **Pragmatic**. It is really exciting.

Whilst I have never been an academic person, and never went to university (I have always preferred to "go out and do stuff") I have recognised over the last year that Psychology plays such a vital role in Enterprise Transformation (for good or bad) and so in February 2014 I began a BSc (Honours) Psychology degree with The Open University. It is really exciting.

MBTI

My MBTI is a split between **INTJ** and **INTP**.

INTJ - Sometimes referred to as the "Architect," or the "Strategist," people with INTJ personalities are highly analytical, creative and logical.

Strengths: Enjoys theoretical and abstract concepts. High expectations. Good at listening. Takes criticism well. Self-confident and hard-working.

Weaknesses: Can be overly analytical and judgmental. Very perfectionistic. Dislikes talking about emotions. Sometimes seems callous or insensitive.

INTP - People who score as INTP are often described as quiet and analytical. They enjoy spending time alone, thinking about how things work and coming up with solutions to problems. INTPs have a rich inner world and would rather focus their attention on their internal thoughts rather than the external world. They typically do not have a wide social circle, but they do tend to be close to a select group of people.

Strengths: Logical and objective. Abstract thinker. Independent. Loyal and affectionate with loved ones.

Weaknesses: Difficult to get to know. Can be insensitive. Prone to self-doubt. Struggles to follow rules. Has trouble expressing feelings.

DISC

My DISC Profile is 7414 and categorised as **Result-Oriented.**

Result-Oriented people display self-confidence, which some may interpret as arrogance. They actively seek opportunities that test and develop their abilities to accomplish results. Result-Oriented persons like difficult tasks, competitive situations, unique assignments, and "important" positions. They undertake responsibilities with an air of self-importance and display self-satisfaction once they have finished.

Result-Oriented people tend to avoid constraining factors such as direct controls, time-consuming details, and routine work. Because they are forceful and direct, they may have difficulties with others. Result-Oriented people prize their independence and may become restless where involved with group activities or committee work. Although Result-Oriented people generally prefer to work alone, they may persuade others to support their efforts especially when completing routine activities.

Result-Oriented people are quick-thinkers, and they are impatient and fault-finding with those who are not They evaluate others on their ability to get results. Result Oriented people are determined and persistent even in the face of antagonism. They take command of the situation when necessary, whether or not they are in charge. In their uncompromising drive for results, they may appear blunt and uncaring.

Belbin

Belbin categorises me as a **Plant** (Creative and inventive individuals, Plants are the ones in the team most likely to come up with new ideas and suggestions. The name comes from Dr Belbin's original research. It was discovered that there was no initial spark of an idea in a team unless a creative person was "planted" in each team) and a **Shaper** (Shapers are people who challenge the team to improve. They are dynamic and usually extroverted people who enjoy stimulating others, questioning norms, and finding the best approaches for solving problems.).

Putting MBTI, DISC and Belbin together just about sums me up to a tee.

Different people have different profiles, and different profiles fit into different roles in different ways. We all kind of know this but do we ever take it into account?

> # KEYPOINT:
>
> Use people for the type of person they are, not the type of person you want them to be. If we were all the same, nothing would ever get done.

Questions to Ponder

- What are the MBTI, DISC and Belbin profiles of the people in your Enterprise?
- Do they all suit their roles?
- Have you ever found someone to be a "difficult person" or a "loose cannon"?
- If so, did their MBTI/DISC/Belbin profile taken into account?

PF2 introduces the Companies and Frameworks that are part of the Pragmatic Family.

The Introduction section of PF2 introduces the companies that are part of the Pragmatic Family.

Pragmatic 365 is a non-profit research company. Pragmatic EC is a consulting company.

Most consultancies only want to sell you fish.
Pragmatic will teach you how to fish.

Use Pragmatic Frameworks (for free) to improve your Enterprise.

PEAF Certified training, provides everything to enable you to adopt PEAF.

PEAF Focused Workshops, allow you to focus on specific areas.

Access to the Pragmatic Publishing Platform is granted by graduating from an Instructor led course.

P3 allows Enterprises to easily produce and maintain their own Frameworks and publish them to books, their intranet and mobile devices.

P3 is a component based authoring system.

Appendix

The Frameworks section of PF2 introduces the Frameworks that are part of the Pragmatic Family.

To understand the whole, you first must understand the whole.

The Pragmatic Family of Frameworks are all about Connecting the DOTS™.

Pragmatic Frameworks are Pragmatic, Well-defined, Complete, Interlocking, Inheritable and Extensible.

Pragmatic Frameworks were designed to be modified.

PEAF inherits from POET inherits from PF2.

PEFF provides the Context for POET provides the Context for PEAF.

Pragmatic Frameworks were mostly influenced by the thinking of Deming and Zachman.

POET grew out of things originally in PEAF, that applied to all of the Transformation space, not just the EA part.

PEFF - The Pragmatic Enterprise Fundamentals Framework.

PEEF allows an Enterprise to define and put in place fundamental Ontologies used throughout an Enterprise.

POET - The Pragmatic Operating model for Enterprise Transformation.

POET allows you to Strategically guide the Tactical changes, to the Transformation capability of your Enterprise.

POET allows an Enterprise to take a coherent and holistic view of the Transformation part of your Enterprise.

POET allows an Enterprise to Tactically improve parts of Transformation, in the context of the Strategic whole.

PEAF - The Pragmatic Enterprise Architecture Framework.

POET allows you to Strategically guide the Tactical changes, to the Transformation capability of your Enterprise.

PEAF allows an Enterprise to take a coherent and holistic view of the Strategising and Roadmapping (EA) Transformation phases of your Enterprise.

PEAF allows an Enterprise to Tactically improve parts of EA, in the context of the Strategic whole.

PTMC - The Pragmatic Transformation Maturity Canvas.

PTMC allows an Enterprise to assess the fitness of the Transformation Capability of your Enterprise.

The PTMC allows an Enterprise to Strategically assess its Transformation Capability, so it can Tactically mature it.

The PTMC allows you to Pragmatically assess the Transformation capability of your Enterprise.

POED - The Pragmatic Operating model for Enterprise Direction.

POED allows you to Strategically guide the Tactical changes, to the Direction capability of your Enterprise.

POEO - The Pragmatic Operating model for Enterprise Operation.

POEO allows you to Strategically guide the Tactical changes, to the Operation capability of your Enterprise.

POES - The Pragmatic Operating model for Enterprise Support.

POES allows you to Strategically guide the Tactical changes, to the Support capability of your Enterprise.

PEEF - The Pragmatic Enterprise Engineering Framework.

POET allows you to Strategically guide the Tactical changes, to the Transformation capability of your Enterprise.

POET and PEAF bridge the chasm between Zachman and TOGAF.

People incorrectly think Pragmatic Frameworks are either too high level and conceptual or incorrectly think they are too large and detailed.

Key Framework comparison criteria: Strategic vs Project, Enterprise vs IT, Detail vs Usability.

Raw Scores given by Pragmatic show PEAF in the lead.

The EA framework you choose, depends on what you want from your EA framework.

If you favour Project guidance and Detail, rather than Strategic guidance and Usability – then TOGAF is clearly for you.

If you favour Strategic guidance and Usability, rather than Project guidance and Detail – then PEAF is clearly for you.

PEAF provides the Bootstrap to kickstart your TOGAF adoption.

PEAF provides the 20% (fundamentals) that yields 80% of the benefit. TOGAF provides the 80% (details), that yields 20% of the benefit.

PEAF covers the whole of TOGAF and more.

Start with POET and PEAF, and then move on to TOGAF if required.

POET provides an Operating model for how Zachman, TOGAF, PEAF, COBIT, ITIL (and all other Transformation frameworks) relate to each other.

Frameworks that span multiple domains (Transformation, Operation and Support) fragment the Enterprise.

POET/PEAF/PEEF provides the 20% (fundamentals) that yields 80% of the benefit. TOGAF provides the 80% (details), that yields 20% of the benefit.

The trend for TOGAF is falling. The Trend for PEAF is rising.

You can't change what you don't understand.
You can't understand what you can't see.

In the Zachman Framework/Ontology, the Deployer perspective is missing.

POET and PEAF greatly extends what Zachman provides.

Zachman's Architect and Engineer rows are wrong, because Architecture and Engineering can be performed at any row.

Zachman's Why and How columns, only equate to the Motivation and Actions of MAGMA.
Why and How are also questions answered by moving up and down the rows, not columns.

Zachman's top two rows equate to MAGIC but the lower down you go the more IT specific it becomes.

Zachman's (corrected) perspectives and models can be mapped to the Phases and Levels of POET.

Use POET as a conceptual guide.

Use POET as a Contextual /
Conceptual guide.
Use PEAF as a logical guide.

The Appendix section contains
information on the background of
PF2, POET, PEAF and the author.

Use POET and PEAF to make sure
you don't make the mistakes that
cause 90% of all EA initiatives to fail.

Use people for the type of person they are, not the type of person you want them to be. If we were all the same, nothing would ever get done.

All Pragmatic books contain a Keypoint section.

www.Pragmatic365.org is the official source for all PF2/POET/PEAF related materials, and is constantly evolving.

Pragmatic EA is a non-profit research company, dedicated to developing Best Practice in relation to the structure and transformation of Enterprises.

Sources

- Book cover: Tropical Storm Lee - NASA/NOAA GOES Project Science Team.
- Stereogram used on "Hitting the Wall" produced by Easy Stereogram Builder - www.easystereogrambuilder.com
- "Brain Function with gears and cogs" used on the "Slaves to Psychology" graphic from BigStock - www.bigstockphoto.com/search/digitalista
- Technical Debt - www.wikipedia.org/wiki/Technical_debt
- Zachman Framework - www.wikipedia.org/wiki/Zachman_Framework
- TOGAF (The Open Group Architecture Framework) - www.opengroup.org/togaf/
- Business Motivation Model - www.omg.org/spec/BMM/
- Enhanced Business Motivation Model - www.MotivationModel.com
- ITIL (IT Infrastructure Library) - www.itil-officialsite.com
- COBIT (Control Objectives for Information and Related Technology) - www.wikipedia.org/wiki/Cobit

Resources

- www.Pragmatic365.org is the official source for all **Pragmatic** related materials.

Here is listed various sources and references to things referred to in the **Pragmatic** Frameworks.

You can always access the most up to date material online at www.Pragmatic365.org.

> ## KEYPOINT:
>
> www.Pragmatic365.org is the official source for all PF2/POET/PEAF related materials, and is constantly evolving.

Pragmatic 365

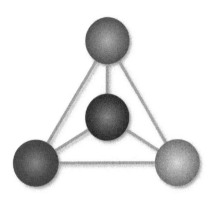

CONNECTING THE DOTS

KEYPOINT:

Pragmatic EA is a non-profit research company, dedicated to developing Best Practice in relation to the structure and transformation of Enterprises.